AMERICAN HOME

Stephanie Alison Walker

BROADWAY PLAY PUBLISHING INC
New York
www.broadwayplaypublishing.com
info@broadwayplaypublishing.com

Cover art by Allison Gorjian

First edition: October 2022
I S B N: 978-0-88145-952-4

Book design: Marie Donovan
Page make-up: Adobe InDesign
Typeface: Palatino

AMERICAN HOME was the winner of the 2011 Blue Ink Playwriting Contest given by American Blues Theater.

AMERICAN HOME had a workshop production at Concordia University in October 2013, directed by Meghan Beals in cooperation with Chicago Dramatists.

AMERICAN HOME premiered at the Fremont Centre Theatre in South Pasadena, California, on 26 August 2017, produced by Little Candle Productions (Allison Darby Gorjian, Artistic Director). The cast and creative contributors were:

DANA WASHINGTON	Ozioma Akagha
MIKE WASHINGTON	Jono Eiland
FLORENCE RAINWATER	Bette Smith
PREACHER PAULA	Jessica Kay Temple
Ensemble	Jennifer Adler, Marc Barnes, Mel Green, Iman Nazemzadeh, Jon Snow, & Caroline Westheimer

Director	Kate Woodruff
Stage Manager	Betsy Roth
Assistant Stage Manager	Andrew Maldonado
Lighting Designer	Rob Van Guelpen
Costume Designer	Paula Deming
Prop Designer	Ellie Roth

CHARACTERS & SETTING

DANA WASHINGTON, 32. *Her inherent optimism stems from the fact that she never had to worry about money. Until now.*

MIKE WASHINGTON, 34. DANA's *husband. A computer programmer. Up to his eyeballs in debt. Terrified of poverty having grown up poor.*

FLORENCE RAINWATER, 80. *A widow who is losing her home to foreclosure.*

ROBBIE WEST, 30/40s. *Special deputy in the Washtenaw County Sheriff Department. Wants to help people. Does not enjoy kicking them out of their homes.*

PROSPERITY PREACHER PAULA, 40s. *A female prosperity preacher in Tampa Bay, Florida.*

DIANE ZURICH, *news anchor. Takes herself very seriously.*

HUGO STORM, 40s. *News anchor. Thinks very highly of himself.*

ESCROW OFFICER, *chipper and seems to really like her job.*

BUYER 1, *a 30-something buying her first house and expecting her first baby.*

BUYER 2, *a 30-something buying his first house and expecting his first baby.*

LORETTA BENSON, 50s. *Woman who faxed a suicide note to her mortgage company.*

JIM BENSON, *50s.* LORETTA's *husband. Heartbroken, grief-stricken.*

DANA'S MOM, *60s. Lives far away & worries about her daughter.*

REALTOR, *trying to survive the downturn like everyone else.*

JENNY LANCASTER, *53. Woman who chained herself to her house to try to stop the foreclosure.*

GUY, *40s.* MIKE's *boss. Wants to be liked.*

NANCY, *40s.* GUY's *wife. Privileged and pragmatic.*

CREDITOR 1
NINA SING
MARCUS JONES
FANNIE MAE
CREDITOR 2

5 *female actors required, 4 male actors required; suggested doubling:*

DIANE ZURICH / ESCROW OFFICER / BUYER 1/
   ENSEMBLE 4
DANA'S MOM / NANCY / CREDITOR 1 / LORETTA /
   JENNY LANCASTER / NINA SING / ENSEMBLE 2
MARCUS JONES / FANNIE MAE / ENSEMBLE 1
ROBBIE WEST / JIM / BUYER 2 / ENSEMBLE 5
HUGO STORM / GUY / CREDITOR 2 / REALTOR/
   ENSEMBLE 3

Time: 2008/2009 (the beginning of the housing crisis)

Places:
A mid-century modern house in Los Angeles, California
A modest house in Ann Arbor, Michigan
A mega-church in Fort Lauderdale, Florida
and various other settings

AUTHOR'S NOTE

It has been estimated that as many as 10 million families lost their homes to foreclosure as a result of the 2008 housing crisis. The foreclosure crisis created, in my opinion, an epidemic of shame. Shame kept people from talking to the banks. Shame led victims of the crisis to take their own lives. Shame made them think they deserved it or had no other choice.

For us, we were afraid of what would happen next and too ashamed that we were here in the first place to even talk about it. Then my mom, who is a Realtor, told us that most people facing foreclosures feel that same shame and it keeps them from taking any constructive action.

We knew we had to talk about it. We had to find a way to be vulnerable and own our story. It's what saved us. Because shame doesn't want to be recognized, so as soon as you start talking about that thing that is causing so much shame, you are set free. We deeply were ashamed. We were afraid. And we knew we had to talk. To each other. To the bank. To our family and friends. And to anyone who would listen. It is what set us free.

We lost our house and all of our money, but we were lucky because we didn't lose each other. Millions upon millions of Americans lost so much during this crisis. This play is for them. For the people who lost their homes and so much more. It's for those people who lost loved ones. It is for those who helped people through the very worst by providing meals, help with packing, emotional support, a place to stay or an empathetic ear. It's for those people who still struggle today. Who feel they'll never climb out from beneath their crushing debt and financial hardship. I hope you never feel alone. Because you're not. You're not. You're really not. It's your shame that wants you to feel that way. Don't let it win. This play is for Addie Polk—who inspired the storyline of Florence Rainwater. Florence's story got the ending Addie didn't. This is for Addie's family and all the Addies in the world. May we never forget these stories. May we all find ways to be like Robbie and take care of each other. Take a stand. Take a breath.

NOTE ON MUSIC

For performance of copyrighted songs, arrangements or recordings referenced in this play, permission of the copyright owner(s) must be obtained.

For Bob

ACT ONE

Dreams of Houses

(*Lights up on a young woman who looks thirty but moves with childlike abandonment. This is* DANA WASHINGTON. *She is forming clouds with her breath, like a child blowing bubbles. But instead of bubbles, clouds appear.*)

(*The* ENSEMBLE *watches her. They respond to each cloud.*)

(DANA *creates one cloud.*)

ENSEMBLE: Ooooooh!

(DANA *creates another cloud.*)

ENSEMBLE: Ahhhhhhh!

(DANA *creates a third cloud.*)

ENSEMBLE: Oooooooh!

(DANA *admires her clouds.*)

DANA: When I grow up, I'm going to have a house made of clouds. The floors, the furniture, the ceiling… clouds. So soft and fluffy, no one will ever get hurt in my house. (*She makes another cloud.*)

ENSEMBLE: Aaaaaaaah….

ENSEMBLE 1: (*As a small child*) When I grow up, I'm gonna have a house built into a mountain side where no one can find me and where I'll know it's raining before anyone else.

ENSEMBLE 2: *(As a teenager)* When I grow up I will live in a casita in Spain. In a small village. Where I am the only American and I speak solamente Español.

(The ENSEMBLE *blurts out a few Spanish words/phrases here in response. Such as: "Hola!" "Como estás?" "Vino tinto!")*

ENSEMBLE 3: *(As a twenty-something)* When I grow up, I'll live on a boat and sail the world communing with nature, drinking rum, writing novels and collecting experiences, not things.

ENSEMBLE 4: *(Excited to join in…as a twenty something)* Oooh! When I grow up I will live in a house made of stained glass. *(Painting the picture)* Light filtering through and refracting in the most sensational ways. Changing perspective by the moment. The sun will live to shine its light through my stained glass house. To send its rays down to earth and through my bedroom window where I sleep like a kaleidoscope. My body painted in refracted light. Jewel tones and heavenly hues.

DANA: *(As present day)* When I grow up, I will have a house with a two-car garage, built-in bookshelves and a fireplace in every room. We'll sit and watch the fire, my husband and I… the man of my dreams. The perfect man who is flawed just perfectly. Because we all have flaws. The trick is to choose the right flaws. Flaws that over time charm you. Like a stupid joke.

*(*ENSEMBLE *becomes a cocktail party. Chitter chatter)*

DANA: The man of my dreams will tell the same joke— his favorite—to everyone he meets:)

*(*MIKE—*the man of* DANA*'s dreams—enters. He addresses the* ENSEMBLE*/cocktail party. She observes.)*

MIKE: *(Deadpan)* Why did the monkey fall out of the tree? *(Beat)* Because he was dead.

(No one laughs. Except for DANA. MIKE *turns towards her. Smiles. Then moves closer to her.)*

*(*ENSEMBLE *watches this love at first sight moment. The chemistry between them is palpable. They are drawn powerfully towards each other.)*

DANA: *(Eyes on the man of her dreams…as a woman in love)* When I grow up I will live in a house made of moss. That lives and breathes and grows a little each day. I will love my house made of moss. I will live there with my husband. The man of my dreams who tells the same stupid joke every day. *(She moves towards* MIKE.*)* When I marry the man of my dreams, no house will be able to contain our love. We may as well live in a cardboard box. Because it won't matter.

*(*DANA *and* MIKE *face each other, hold hands as though exchanging the following as marriage vows.)*

DANA: We could live in a tunnel.

MIKE: A balloon.

DANA: An empty water drain.

MIKE: A drop of rain.

DANA: As long as we have each other. *(Letting them in on a secret)* But still I dream of houses.

The Widow of Ann Arbor

(A phone rings loudly. Fills the theatre. This sound effect might be created by the ENSEMBLE.*)*

(Lights come up as the phone continues to ring.)

(Seated in an ancient Lazy Boy recliner is FLORENCE RAINWATER *[90]. She is wrapped tightly in a blanket and holds the ringing telephone in her lap.)*

(The ringing continues. She looks at the phone.)

(She picks it up. The ringing stops. She says nothing.)

(She listens. The voice on the other end echoes through the theatre.)

FANNIE MAE: Hello? *(No response)* Florence Rainwater? Mrs Florence Rainwater? Hello? *(Listening)* Is anyone there? Ma'am, this is an urgent, confidential matter and I need to confirm that you are who I think you are. Who we hope to reach. Mrs Florence Rainwater, that is. Is this you? *(No response)* Ma'am? *(Beat)* I can hear you breathing.

(FLORENCE hangs up.)

(The phone rings again. Almost immediately. She picks up and hangs up. She stands, reluctantly abandons her Lazy Boy and follows the telephone cord off stage.)

Bubbles Always Burst

(HUGO STORM and DIANE ZURICH take center stage.)

DIANE ZURICH: In today's real estate news—

HUGO STORM: You know we finally pulled the trigger on that Palm Beach house.

DIANE ZURICH: Yes. You told me.

HUGO STORM: Real excited about it.

DIANE ZURICH: Can I—?

HUGO STORM: Go ahead.

DIANE ZURICH: In today's real estate news, the word of the day is "bubble".

(ENSEMBLE might take out their bubbles and begins to blow them.)

HUGO STORM: Or is it "boom"?

DIANE ZURICH: No, it's "bubble", dear.

HUGO STORM: Well…

DIANE ZURICH: Something that lacks firmness, solidity or *reality*.

HUGO STORM: Let's not get carried away. Things might be slowing down a bit, but that doesn't mean that we're in a bubble. Plenty of experts say—

DIANE ZURICH: "A state of booming economic activity that often ends in a sudden collapse." Are we experiencing a real estate bubble? Experts say, "Yes".

(DIANE ZURICH *annoyed by the bubbles. If they come near her, she waves them out of her way and attempts to cover her annoyance.*)

HUGO STORM: My Real Estate agent says, "No".

DIANE ZURICH: Of course he does.

HUGO STORM: She. (*Under his breath*) Sexist.

(*This gets a laugh from the* ENSEMBLE. DIANE ZURICH *again expertly covers her annoyance and soldiers on.*)

DIANE ZURICH: A recent report published by the Center for American Progress titled, "The End of the Great American Housing Boom," warns of the inevitable burst—

HUGO STORM: Fear mongering. That's all it is, folks.

DIANE ZURICH: Senior economist for the Center for American Progress, Christian Weller, says…

(ENSEMBLE 1 *stands.*)

ENSEMBLE 1: "The economy has been dependent almost like an addict on people cashing out the equity in their homes." (*Sits*)

DIANE ZURICH: And as housing prices fall, access to affordable credit becomes more difficult creating challenges for would-be homeowners in need of a mortgage. *(Beat. To* HUGO STORM*)* The party, as they say, is over.

HUGO STORM: Well…we'll see.

*(*MIKE *&* DANA *enter, hand in hand…they are looking at a house.)*

DIANE ZURICH: *(To* HUGO STORM*)* You know what happens to bubbles, don't you?

*(*ENSEMBLE *bursts their bubbles.)*

Mike & Dana Washington Fall in Love… with a House

*(*MIKE *and* DANA *[30s] are standing in the house of their dreams for the first time. She explores the space with love in her eyes.)*

MIKE: *(To the audience)* I grew up in a trailer park in Iowa. Didn't have enough money ever for anything. That's how it felt. Like I'd never get what I wanted. My friends would see a toy they wanted, ask their parents for it and like magic it would be theirs. By the time I was ten I had two paper routes and an ulcer. An ulcer. At ten years old. I never knew what it felt like to just want something and make it your own. To want something, reach into your wallet, pull out the cash and own it.

I was the first in my family to go to college. Now I make two hundred dollars an hour as a computer programmer and when I want something, I make it mine.

DANA: I love it, Mike! I love it so much. I love, love, love, love, love, love, love, love, love it!

*(*MIKE *watches* DANA *as she floats and spins through the house. Discovering)*

DANA: So much space! It's so open. Wide open-
I've always wanted vaulted ceilings and built-in
bookshelves! And this view…look! You can see all the
way to Big Bear!

(DANA *takes in the view.* MIKE *joins her. Holds her hand,
lacing their fingers)*

DANA: I can't believe this hasn't sold yet.

MIKE: Telephone wires.

DANA: Well, it is a city. Of course there are telephone
wires.

MIKE: But they're so close. I feel like I could reach out
and *(He reaches out.)* Touch them.

(DANA *pirouettes through the living room.)*

DANA: *(While pirouetting)* So. Much. Space!

MIKE: If you start doing leaps, I will leave.

(DANA *leaps.)*

(MIKE *turns to leave.)*

*(She jumps onto his back and squeals. Her enthusiasm
infects him against his will. She slides down his back and he
pulls her towards him. They laugh together.)*

(She kisses him. Quickly. Passionately. Then releases him.)

(His smile turns slowly into pain. She notices.)

DANA: What's wrong, Babe?

MIKE: My stomach.

DANA: I told you. The peppers. Shouldn't have eaten
them.

MIKE: No. It's…

DANA: You hate the house.

MIKE: I was hoping to hate it.

DANA: You were hoping to hate it?

MIKE: So we wouldn't have to buy it.

DANA: I thought you wanted a house.

MIKE: I do. But—

DANA: We've looked and looked and looked and looked/

MIKE: I know.

DANA: /and we haven't seen anything even close to this—

MIKE: I know.

(A beat. DANA *walks towards the view.)*

DANA: And I know it's not what we budgeted, but we were being really conservative. I can take on more translation projects. We can tighten our budget everywhere else. I know it'll be tight, but…this is what you do, right? When you find 'the one.' You do everything you can to grab a hold of that piece of earth and then you dig in, plant yourself and spread your roots so you can thrive. And I feel it. This is it. Sometimes you just have to throw your hat over the wall.

(No response. MIKE's *thinking.* DANA *watches him.)*

MIKE: We said if we didn't like this one then we'd stop looking. We agreed.

DANA: I remember.

MIKE: No more open houses. No more looking. This is it.

DANA: Right.

MIKE: But if you think about it, we'd be getting this house for a great price. I mean, it was just reduced.

DANA: Yep.

MIKE: We've seen a lot of houses.

DANA: A lot.

MIKE: This is the first house you have…ballerina-d in.

DANA: This is true.

MIKE: And these views. These fucking views. I look at these views and I think there is no way this house could depreciate. Not with these views. *(Quick beat)* Maybe we can get those lines buried.

DANA: This might sound weird, but it feels like it's already ours. Like we already live here. Like… like…

MIKE: Like we've *always* lived here.

(Slight beat. DANA smiles at this.)

DANA: Our dining room table is right here. Can you see it? We're hosting a fabulous dinner party with all of our friends. Our sofa is right here. This is where we sit and read and snuggle and just gaze out at the view of the mountains and twinkly lights… And here… Our bed. This room. This is our room. This is where we lie in bed together looking at the moon. Can you see it? This is where we have breakfast in bed and where—

MIKE: Where we make babies.

(A beat. This sinks in.)

DANA: You really mean that?

(MIKE nods. DANA rushes to him and kisses him. Then…)

DANA: This room over here is where our baby sleeps. And come on! How much do you want that fireplace?!

MIKE: I want to make love to you in front of the fire.

DANA: On a soft rug?

MIKE: On a soft rug.

(MIKE kisses DANA. A sweet little kiss.)

MIKE: You want this house?

(DANA *nods. Holding back tears*)

MIKE: I want you to have everything you want.

DANA: Does that mean—

MIKE: Yeah.

DANA: You want it too?

(*Off* MIKE's *look:*)

DANA: I knew it! I knew you loved it like me.

MIKE: Shit.

DANA: We're living on the skinny branches, baby!

MIKE: Those views…

DANA: I know.

MIKE: I don't *want* to want this, but…

DANA: But…have we ever regretted taking a chance on something we really believed in?

MIKE: We got married.

DANA: Exactly.

MIKE: Okay.

DANA: Okay? So we're going for it.

MIKE: We're going for it.

(MIKE *grabs* DANA's *hand. They squeeze.*)

MIKE: Ready?

(DANA *and* MIKE *inhale.*)

Prosperity Preacher Paula Challenges Her Parishoners

(Lights up on PROSPERITY PREACHER PAULA—*a small powerhouse of a woman.)*

(She is larger than life. Her diminutive frame transcends expectation. She is everywhere.)

(Center stage, on two giant JumboTron screens, in living rooms and nail salons across America.)

(She has spared no expense with the production values of her ministry. She is bathed in gorgeous, heavenly light.)

(Her sermon is accompanied by the soft sounds of a live band—the accompaniment lifts her words up to the congregation and serves them on a gold platter…in stereo surround.)

(The ENSEMBLE *is her congregation. They interact and ad lib throughout her sermon. Imagine a diverse congregation.)*

PREACHER PAULA: Are you ready? Are you ready to accept the Lord's blessings?! Come on! I know you are. There was a time I believed I didn't deserve the time of day from the Lord. I didn't even know how to talk to Him. It's true. I didn't think I deserved happiness. I KNEW I didn't deserve to be prosperous. But you know what? That wasn't never up to me. Whether or not I was deserving of Him. That was up to God. Whether or not you deserve something…leave that to God. What I didn't know then that I know now— God wants us to be prosperous. The Lord wants his most faithful to be rich. He wants you to live a prosperous life. He wants you to have that family you long for. He wants you to find your soul mate. He wants you to luxuriate in the home of your dreams. That big, beautiful house you dream of. Oh, yes. God is dreaming of that house for you. He dreams so big for you. Don't you dare insult him by playing small.

Y'all know what I mean, don't you? He wants you
to be prosperous, and you know where that begins?
On the inside. In here. Start listening to what you tell
yourself. Do not make the mistake I did for so much
of my life and tell yourself that you aren't worthy. Do
not disrespect God by listening to that nagging voice
that tells you don't deserve His blessings. That voice is
not the voice of God so don't you give it any airtime.
Change the channel. Just like that. You change it until
you land on that channel where all you hear is the
voice of God inside your head telling you the truth:
You are worthy. Psalm 37:4 "Delight yourself also in
the lord and he will give you the desires of your heart."
Yes, He wants us to prosper. But prosperity isn't a
right. It's a reward.

What does this mean? It means ya'll need to stop
asking whether or not you are deserving and instead
ask whether or not you are making choices on a
daily basis to *earn* that prosperity. If you want God's
blessings you gotta first give God something to work
with. Give Him something to work with. You know
where I'm going with this, don't you?

If you want love, you need to give love. If you want
happiness, you need to start by giving joy to the people
around you. If what you want is a house, you need to
give first to the house of God. You need to give God
something to work with! Amen?

ENSEMBLE: Amen!

PREACHER PAULA: You sow that seed and watch it
grow. It happened for me, it can happen for you.
I know pain. I know the pain of loneliness. I'm an
orphan. I know loneliness. I know abandonment. I
know abuse and starvation. I know what it's like to
live on food stamps and sleep on the ground without
a roof over my head. I know what it's like to live for
nothing except your next fix to numb that unbearable

pain. I know what it's like to wake up in a hospital bed on death's door. I know what it's like to be told by the doctor that you will never be able to have children of your own. I know. Oh, I know. I know what it's like to be given a mission from God. To be saved. To accept Jesus. To reinvent myself. To be given another chance. To stand in the unknown and feel more confidence than ever before in my entire life. I know what it's like to give myself to the Word. I also know abundance. The joy in saving others. Unlimited blessings upon my life. A mission. A purpose. That first time I sowed a seed, I had nothing. I was living on food stamps. I had nothing. And yet, I planted the seed. It didn't even make sense. Why a thousand dollars? I can't tell you why, but it worked. I'm here to tell you if it worked for me, it can work for you. But if you want the abundance of God's love, you have to first give God something to work with. Give him something to work with. Give God—what?

ENSEMBLE: Something to work with!

PREACHER PAULA: AMEN!

The Widow & The Deputy

(A doorbell rings and rings.)

(FLORENCE enters wrapped in a blanket and wearing mittens and a hat. She moves across her house to the door as though there's another person to consider.)

FLORENCE: Hold your pants on. I'm comin'!

(FLORENCE opens the door to ROBBIE WEST [30s/40s] dressed properly for the cold…in his Sheriff's Deputy jacket.)

FLORENCE: Robbie! Thank your soul for comin'.

(ROBBIE enters carrying a huge stack of mail.)

ROBBIE: It's no trouble, Mrs Rainwater. You can always call me. I've always said that.

FLORENCE: I know. You're a good boy.

ROBBIE: Your mail.

FLORENCE: Oh, you can just set it over there.

ROBBIE: It's a big stack.

FLORENCE: Junk.

ROBBIE: It's not all junk. You should go through it.

FLORENCE: There's nothing interesting in the mail anymore.

ROBBIE: Well, maybe not interesting. But bills. Bills still come in the mail.

FLORENCE: Like I said. Just set it down. Leave my troubles to me.

(ROBBIE *holds onto the mail.*)

(FLORENCE *settles herself into her Lazy Boy and tries to cover herself with a blanket.* ROBBIE *tries to help her.*)

ROBBIE: How long you been without heat?

FLORENCE: Oh, I don't know. A couple days. *(She picks up her Reader's Digest.)*

ROBBIE: A couple days?! Why didn't you call me sooner?

FLORENCE: I don't like being a bother.

ROBBIE: You're not a bother. Living in the cold like this is dangerous.

FLORENCE: I'm tough. How did I get to live so long? Because I'm tough. Anyway, you're here now.

ROBBIE: I never see you around town anymore.

FLORENCE: Too much trouble. Going out. Getting all ready. Especially in the cold. You gotta layer. Takes a lot of effort. And that car out there don't start so easy in the cold. It sleeps out in the garage like a baby with a blanket on its engine. It has it better than some people. A roof over its head, a blanket on its engine and still it doesn't start for me. It's stubborn. It doesn't want to go out in the cold. Guess we have that in common.

ROBBIE: Well, if you ever want to go out…you know get out of the house…go to the store, see a friend…I can come by an' pick you up. I wouldn't mind.

FLORENCE: I'm a good driver.

ROBBIE: I know you are. It's just you said you didn't want to drive in the cold—

FLORENCE: It's not about not wanting to drive- it's about not wanting the hassle of getting ready.

ROBBIE: Okay.

FLORENCE: I like driving.

ROBBIE: Okay.

FLORENCE: I just don't like getting ready.

ROBBIE: I hear ya loud and clear, Florence.

(A beat. FLORENCE *allows the silence to settle the matter.)*

ROBBIE: So.

FLORENCE: So.

ROBBIE: You want me to check the pilot light?

FLORENCE: I already checked the pilot light.

ROBBIE: And?

FLORENCE: It's out.

ROBBIE: Well, then I'll go light it.

FLORENCE: You think I don't know how to light the pilot light? I've been trying to light it and it won't light.

ROBBIE: The gas must be out.

(No response)

ROBBIE: Well, I'll check it just the same. Just to be sure. Maybe I got the magic touch.

FLORENCE: I doubt that.

(ROBBIE hands FLORENCE the stack of mail.)

FLORENCE: I said I didn't want that.

ROBBIE: I know. Still, though. You should go through it. It's a big stack. You might even find something in there like maybe something from the gas company.

FLORENCE: Like what?

ROBBIE: Like a love letter.

FLORENCE: Just go fix my heater and stop being nosey.

(ROBBIE leaves the mail in FLORENCE's hands. Exits. She drops the stack of mail into a wastebasket.)

Mike & Dana Sign at the Dotted Line

(MIKE and DANA sit stiffly in the escrow office opposite the ESCROW OFFICER. She flips through a stack of documents. Organizing. MIKE and DANA wait patiently. Nervously. MIKE is sighing audibly.)

ESCROW OFFICER: Nervous?

DANA: He does that. He forgets to breathe. Especially in times like this.

MIKE: I can't get my breath.

ESCROW OFFICER: Homebuyer's remorse. It's like cold feet at a wedding. Or before the wedding. You know. It's perfectly normal.

(Off MIKE's struggle for air:)

ESCROW OFFICER: There's water at reception.

MIKE: I'm…okay.

DANA: *(To* MIKE*)* I have a bottle of water if you need it.

MIKE: I'm fine. Let's just get this over with.

ESCROW OFFICER: Okay, almost ready.

DANA: I'm usually the one freaking out. You should have seen me the night he proposed. Only time in my life I ever had a panic attack. I literally thought I was dying. Paramedics came and everything.

ESCROW OFFICER: Really?

DANA: It's funny now. But…not then. Poor Mike.

ESCROW OFFICER: *(To* MIKE…*trying not to laugh)* I can't imagine how awful that must have been for you.

MIKE: No, it's okay. It's funny now. It's a good story.

DANA: And I was so lucky you didn't take my panic attack personally and run out on me. *(To* ESCROW OFFICER*)* That's when I knew that I had to marry him. It was like his worst nightmare version of how the proposal would go, but he was so great about it. He just held my hand and said, "Together we can conquer anything. Even marriage".

*(*ESCROW OFFICER *is hanging on her every word. She sighs.)*

ESCROW OFFICER: So romantic.

*(*DANA *takes* MIKE*'s hand and smiles.)*

ESCROW OFFICER goes back to shuffling papers.

ESCROW OFFICER: Okay…this is what we're signing.

*(*ESCROW OFFICER *hoists an enormous stack of documents— each* ENSEMBLE *member hoists their own stack of documents—and drops them in front of* MIKE *and* DANA *[*ENSEMBLE *drops them in unison on the floor in front of their chairs]. The thud of the documents reverberates throughout the theatre.)*

ESCROW OFFICER: Don't be intimidated. It's just paper.

DANA: How long will this take?

ESCROW OFFICER: That depends. Do you want to read them?

(DANA *fans through the huge stack.*)

DANA: People read these?

ESCROW OFFICER: Some people do. But I can sum them up for you. Give you the bottom line of each page. And you can ask questions along the way. That's the most expeditious way…

MIKE: Okay.

ESCROW OFFICER: Wunderbar.

DANA: *(To* MIKE*)* Maybe we should read these…

MIKE: It's all standard.

DANA: But I'm not familiar with "standard". This is all new to me and—

MIKE: *(To* DANA*)* We're either doing this or we're not.

DANA: I know. I just—

MIKE: You want to read all these documents? We'll be here all day. The only part we need to know is the PAY YOUR FUCKING MORTGAGE part.

ESCROW OFFICER: *(Laughing)* That's true. *(Quick beat)* Sorry.

MIKE: Are you having second thoughts now?

DANA: No, I'm on board. I just…you know. Contracts.

MIKE: Dana. I'd really like to just get this over with. Get out of here as fast as possi—

DANA: Okay.

MIKE: Good. We're ready.

ESCROW OFFICER: Magnifique. *(She holds up two pens.)* Okay. Here's how this will go. Mr Washington, you sign first, then pass the page to your wife. Mrs Washington, after you add your signature you'll pass it onto me and I'll double check everything, okay? *(Beat)* Any questions?

DANA: Do I have to sign my full name every time?

ESCROW OFFICER: Yes.

DANA: Does it have to look the same?

ESCROW OFFICER: It should. Yes. *(Beat)* Anything else? *(She looks to MIKE and DANA…)* Okay, then let's—

DANA: *(To ESCROW OFFICER)* Do you think we should do it?

ESCROW OFFICER: Do I think you should…?

DANA: Buy this house.

ESCROW OFFICER: *(Thinks. Chooses words carefully)* Um… I'm afraid that's not a question I'm able to answer.

DANA: No, I know. I just…

MIKE: Let's just—

DANA: Right.

ESCROW OFFICER: I will say, if I may, you got a really great loan here. The bank clearly has confidence in you two. You know, sometimes I worry about people. I do. But, not you.

(ESCROW OFFICER smiles warmly at DANA who seems satisfied by this response.)

(ESCROW OFFICER hands the pens over.)

ESCROW OFFICER: How 'bout some music?

(MIKE and DANA take the pens and begin to sign. And sign and sign.)

(She presses play and we hear the steel drum intro of Bob Marley's Three Little Birds…*and then the first lyrics [As sung by the* ENSEMBLE:]*)*

ENSEMBLE: Don't worry about a thing…cuz every little thing is gonna be all right.

(DANA *visibly relaxes. They listen, sway to the music and sign as* ESCROW OFFICER *quietly sings along to the music.*)

(MIKE *takes* DANA*'s hand and they cross to:*)

Homeowner Bliss

(DANA *and* MIKE*'s new view. They hold each other with coffee cups and look out at their new view.*)

DANA: Wow. This early morning light. The mountains look like a painting.

(DANA *inhales. She exhales. She takes a sip of coffee. She looks at* MIKE. *Who looks happy. Actually happy*)

MIKE: You know, those telephone lines aren't so bad.

DANA: Barely notice them.

MIKE: And it's kind of like…you know character. The mountains, the freeway and the telephone lines. It's all part of the urban landscape.

DANA: Yeah.

MIKE: Are you happy?

DANA: Mike. I'm so happy it scares me.

How to Close Escrow on Your Dreams

(*Music, Jumbotron and Lights up on* PREACHER PAULA *standing with a congregant—*MARCUS JONES. *She holds a piece of paper up overhead.*)

PREACHER PAULA: This is not just an MLS listing sheet, ladies and gentlemen. This is a dream. And this dream belongs to Marcus Jones. (*To* MARCUS) Go ahead, Marcus. Tell them what this is.

MARCUS: It's a house.

PREACHER PAULA: It is indeed a house. A three-bedroom, two bath house.

MARCUS: With a garage.

PREACHER PAULA: A two-car garage.

MARCUS: We only have one car but we could use the extra space for a workshop. My son and me. We like to build things.

PREACHER PAULA: And a yard.

MARCUS: For the kids to play. And be safe.

PREACHER PAULA: And copper plumbing.

MARCUS: That's an important detail. Plumbing can be expensive.

PREACHER PAULA: This is not just a house, Marcus. This is your dream home. Is it not?

MARCUS: I've worked three jobs for the last fifteen years for this.

PREACHER PAULA: Why are you up here, Marcus?

MARCUS: Well, we haven't been able to qualify for a loan. And all we want is just a place of our own.

PREACHER PAULA: Marcus, you've struggled.

MARCUS: Yes.

PREACHER PAULA: I know it. He knows it. And you know something, Marcus? God does not want you to struggle anymore. God wants all his most faithful to be rich. God wants your family to get that house. He wants you to be prosperous. I just know it. I feel it. *(To the congregation)* Don't you feel it?

(They feel it.)

(This hits MARCUS. *His emotion bursts forth.)*

MARCUS: I'm sorry. I just—

PREACHER PAULA: *(Hand on his shoulder)* It's okay. You let it out. Allow His power to work its way through you. Isaiah 54:2 "Enlarge the place of your tent, stretch your tent curtains wide, do not hold back." He wants us to stretch ourselves. To create an expansive life worthy of the love that God gives us. Do not hold back. I know it's scary. I know it's uncomfortable. But that's okay. It's God's will for you to live in prosperity. Not poverty. And how do we do that? How do we do that? I know many of you are dreaming of your very own house just like Marcus here. Yes. So, listen close. What do you do? First, you get out your eraser. I keep one in my pocket to remind me. *(She pulls an eraser out of her pocket.)* We put erasers under each of your chairs today. So reach down and pick up that powerful eraser because I'm about to tell you what you're gonna do with it. You get your eraser out and you erase all those negative thoughts. Do it right now. Erase them. "I have too much debt." Erase. "I'm too old." Erase. "The world isn't fair." Erase. Erase. Erase."I'll never be able to afford that nice house" Erase! Because you know what you're doing with those negative thoughts? Every time you tell yourself you can't afford that house you're dreaming of? You're cursing your life. So you erase that thought before it has a chance to solidify. You erase it once and for all. And you build your thoughts like your dream house. You build it first in your mind. It's there. Just like it's here. *(Referencing the MLS sheet)* This isn't just an MLS listing sheet here, no. This is your house, Marcus. Yours. *(She holds the listing sheet up to God)* Heavenly Father, we call on you to reward one of your most faithful servants. He's not asking for much. Just a place of his own. A little slice of the American Dream.

(PREACHER PAULA kneels. MARCUS kneels.)

PREACHER PAULA: We humble ourselves in your presence. We thank you for your unconditional love. And we humbly ask for your continued blessing.

ENSEMBLE: Amen!

Firing Practice

(GUY *stands in a bathrobe pacing.* NANCY, *his wife, lounges while reading.*)

(GUY *gathers his thoughts. Stops and tries out this line…*)

GUY: This might come as a shock.

(NANCY *looks up from her book.*)

GUY: *(Off her look)* What?

NANCY: I wouldn't…

GUY: Yeah, you're right. It's too…

NANCY: It's just…

GUY: I know.

NANCY: And he'll know what's coming then.

GUY: You've never done this. You don't know…

NANCY: What does the manual say?

GUY: Just the latest HR bullshit.

NANCY: Maybe you should at least read it, dear.

GUY: This is someone I like. Someone I brought in. And now…

NANCY: Nobody's safe in this climate.

(Beat)

GUY: They just bought a house.

NANCY: That is not your fault.

GUY: I gave him hope.

NANCY: How on earth?

GUY: At least the idea of security.

NANCY: *(Scoffing)* Security. *(Beat)* Security is an illusion.

GUY: No one expected this.

NANCY: I wouldn't say that either. It's false comfort.

GUY: No. *I'm* saying it. I'm saying this to you. No one expected this. Did they?

NANCY: I'm sure someone did.

(GUY slumps into a chair.)

GUY: They're trying to have a baby.

NANCY: Well, I'm sure they'll stop trying. For now. Until he's back on his feet. And then they'll try and they'll get pregnant right away and they'll be changing diapers before they know it and everything will be as it should be. *(Beat)* Besides. You have your own responsibilities to worry about. Don't take on more than you need to emotionally. *(She gets up and crosses to GUY. She rubs his shoulders.)* Remember what the Doctor said.

GUY: I know.

NANCY: Maybe you should go in for a treatment tomorrow. You're so tense.

(NANCY rubs GUY's shoulders for a few beats and he relaxes into it.)

GUY: *(Tries again)* I like you, I really do. It's just this goddamned fucking fucked up economy. We got fucked and you happen to be collateral damage. I'm sorry.

NANCY: You should just say what the manual says.

GUY: We are terminating your contract. Thank you for your work. Pack your things and go.

NANCY: Subtract the emotion.

GUY: Subtract the humanity.

NANCY: He'll be fine. He'll find something else. Maybe even something better. *(Short beat)* Crisis is the breeding ground for opportunity.

GUY: Subtraction. That's all this is.

NANCY: Numbers are numbers are numbers. They don't feel. They don't care. They're just numbers.

(GUY stands. Turns and looks at NANCY)

GUY: *(Tries again)* I'm sorry. You might not believe that. But I truly am.

NANCY: *(Role playing as firee)* Sorry for what?

GUY: I will be happy to be a reference for you. Human resources will be in to help you through the exit process.

NANCY: You're firing me?!

GUY: The decision has been made to terminate your contract.

NANCY: Terminate? Why?

GUY: It's not personal. You're a numbers man. You've seen the numbers. You understand.

(Lights shift. MIKE enters and stands opposite GUY. NANCY exits.)

(An intense beat as GUY registers MIKE's presence.)

(MIKE just stands there staring at GUY. He sways a little.)

MIKE: We just bought a house.

(No response)

MIKE: That's not your problem, though.

GUY: You can count on me for a reference. You'll find something else.

MIKE: I'll find something else.

GUY: You'll find something else. Right away. And, like I said, you can count on me for—

MIKE: A reference.

GUY: Yeah.

MIKE: Thanks. *(Beat)* Well, I guess I'll clear out my desk.

GUY: You WILL find something else.

MIKE: And I'm not gonna freak out.

GUY: Good.

MIKE: Cause I can feel myself really wanting to freak out right now.

GUY: But…

MIKE: But I'm not gonna do that.

GUY: Good.

MIKE: It's not personal.

GUY: It's not. It's really not. It's just—

MIKE: The numbers.

GUY: The numbers.

MIKE: The numbers. *(Beat)* The numbers. *(Beat)* GUY: You sure you're okay?

MIKE: This is hard for you, isn't it?

Maybe This Is a Good Thing

(ENSEMBLE *is up surrounding* MIKE.)

ENSEMBLE 2: I'm sorry.

ENSEMBLE 3: So sorry.

ENSEMBLE 4: That sucks.

ENSEMBLE 5: Well, shit.

ENSEMBLE 1: You okay?

ENSEMBLE 2: You okay?

ENSEMBLE 3: You okay?

ENSEMBLE 4: You gonna be okay?

ENSEMBLE 5: You'll be fine.

ENSEMBLE 2: Maybe it's a good thing.

ENSEMBLE 3: Maybe this is just what you needed.

ENSEMBLE 1: Maybe you're like a phoenix and you're about to rise triumphantly from the ashes.

ENSEMBLE 4: Maybe you'll find something even better.

ENSEMBLE 5: People lose their jobs every day.

ENSEMBLE 2: An opportunity. To land the job of your DREAMS.

ENSEMBLE 3: Money isn't everything.

ENSEMBLE 4: Whatever you do, don't panic.

ENSEMBLE 5: Don't start feeling sorry for yourself.

ENSEMBLE 1: I feel sorry for you, but I won't say that to your face.

ENSEMBLE 2: And I won't say that I'm glad it's not me.

ENSEMBLE 5: But I am.

ENSEMBLE 1: You're still young.

ENSEMBLE 2: You're still young.

ENSEMBLE 3: And good looking.

ENSEMBLE 2: You live in America!

ENSEMBLE 4: You have your health.

ENSEMBLE 5: Sell everything. Start over!

ENSEMBLE 4: Get your resume in order.

ENSEMBLE 1: Start calling in favors.

ENSEMBLE 2: Network.

ENSEMBLE 3: Network!

ENSEMBLE 4: Network.

ENSEMBLE 5: Travel the world. Be free.

ENSEMBLE 4: Don't do anything rash.

ENSEMBLE 1: Just stay calm.

ENSEMBLE 3: We're here to help.

ENSEMBLE 2: Whatever you need. Just ask.

ENSEMBLE 1: You gonna be okay?

ENSEMBLE 2: You gonna be okay?

ENSEMBLE 3: You'll be fine. Better than fine.

ENSEMBLE 1: Pat on the back.

ENSEMBLE 2: Pat on the back.

ENSEMBLE 3: A sad smile.

ENSEMBLE 1: An awkward hug.

ENSEMBLE 4: An embrace that says: You're not alone.

ENSEMBLE 5: A shot of whiskey and a hearty "Fuck this!"

ENSEMBLE 2: I'm just glad it's not me.

ENSEMBLE 1: Glad it's not me.

ENSEMBLE 3: So glad it's not me.

ENSEMBLE 4: Do let us know. If there's anything you need.

ENSEMBLE 2: And just remember…

(DANA *enters. She takes* MIKE's *hand.*)

DANA: We'll get through this. Together.

Mortgage Pies

(Lights on HUGO STORM *and* DIANE ZURICH *on their stools in the studio.)*

HUGO STORM: Now here's a proverbial lemons into lemonade story for you.

DIANE ZURICH: I love a good lemons to lemonade story.

HUGO STORM: Don't we all. When single mother of three, Nina Sing, was downsized from her job in the mortgage industry she turned sour apples into sweet apple pie.

DIANE ZURICH: We have Nina. Nina? Ms Sing?

*(*NINA SING *enters holding a pie.)*

NINA SING: Yes. Hello?

HUGO STORM: There she is.

NINA SING: Hi. Can you hear me?

DIANE ZURICH: We hear you, Nina. And we see your beautiful—is that an apple tree behind you?

NINA SING: It is. I have two apple trees on my property.

HUGO STORM: Ah, the tree that saved your house.

NINA SING: Yes. You could say that. Things were scary after I got laid off. I'm a single mother. Three kids to feed. I was stress baking. A lot. Lots of pies. More pies than I could give away.

HUGO STORM: How did you get the idea to start selling them?

NINA SING: My middle daughter. She's eight and not limited by reason. She was convinced we could sell enough pies to save our home. She made a sign— "Buy a pie and save our home." I was worried what the neighbors would think—

HUGO STORM: Sure. Sure.

NINA SING: But then I thought, I haven't had any better ideas. We might as well give it a try.

DIANE ZURICH: And over the course of six months you sold enough pies to save your home from foreclosure?

NINA SING: We did. And I owe it all to my daughter.

HUGO STORM: What a story.

DIANE ZURICH: It's refreshing, honestly. Foreclosure stories are usually so depressing.

HUGO STORM: I don't know about you, but I'm hungry for pie.

DIANE ZURICH: Rumor has it, we have one here in the studio to try.

NINA SING: Yes. They asked me to send one over. I sent you a blackberry pie. We're overrun with blackberries now too.

(ENSEMBLE *brings out a pie with two forks and hands it to* HUGO STORM *who immediately digs in.*)

HUGO STORM: Mmmm…that's good pie.

(NINA SING *smiles proudly.*)

DIANE ZURICH: What's next for you, Ms Sing?

NINA SING: I've been thinking about trying hand pies.

I used to sell mortgages. Now I sell pies.

HUGO STORM: Well, there you have it. It's undeniably tough out there in this downturn, but everyday Americans are still pulling themselves up by their…pie straps.

DIANE ZURICH: When life hits you with sour apples?

HUGO STORM: Make apple pie!

Florence Lies to Robbie

(A doorbell rings and rings.)

*(*FLORENCE *sits in her armchair all bundled up in a hat, blanket, scarf and mittens.)*

ROBBIE: *(Thru the door)* Mrs Rainwater? Mrs Rainwater! It's me. Robbie.

FLORENCE: What is it, Robbie?!

ROBBIE: *(Thru door)* Are you okay? I tried calling but your phone's turned off.

FLORENCE: I'm fine! Just fine!

ROBBIE: *(Thru door)* Is your heat back on?

FLORENCE: Yes. Thank you. I got that all taken care of. Thank you for checking.

ROBBIE: *(Thru door)* I could build a fire for you. If you want!

FLORENCE: No, Robbie. I'm fine! *(Beat)* I'm about to take a bath.

ROBBIE: *(Thru door)* You sure you're okay?

FLORENCE: Jiminy Christmas. Yes. I'm fine, Robbie. Stop fussing.

ROBBIE: *(Thru door)* Okay. If you say so.

FLORENCE: I do. And I'm going to take my bath now. So…good bye.

ROBBIE: *(Thru door)* Okay, Mrs Rainwater. Have a nice bath!

*(*FLORENCE *sits in her armchair, just staring at the front door.)*

Dana Washington Pees on a Stick

(The phone rings.)

(DANA runs into the room carrying a stick from a pregnancy test. She grabs the phone excitedly.)

DANA: Hello?!

CREDITOR: Mrs Washington?

DANA: Sorry. Yes?

CREDITOR: Is this Mrs Washington?

DANA: Yes. Can I help you?

CREDITOR: I'm calling on behalf of Chase Manhattan Bank.

DANA: Oh, I'm not interested.

CREDITOR: This isn't a sales call, ma'am. This is an urgent matter.

DANA: Have you ever taken an at home pregnancy test?

CREDITOR: I'm sorry?

DANA: I just peed on the stick and two lines appeared. But one line is a little weaker than the other. But they're both there. I'm pretty sure that means I'm pregnant. Right?

CREDITOR: Uh…

DANA: I tried it twice and I had the same result both times. Have you ever—

CREDITOR: Ma'am, this is—

DANA: I'm pretty sure this means I'm pregnant. I'm pregnant!

CREDITOR: Ma'am…

DANA: Oh my god, oh my god.

CREDITOR: Congratulations.

DANA: Is this a sales call?

CREDITOR: No, Ma'am. This is not a sales call. We're calling to collect payment.

DANA: Collect payment for what?

CREDITOR: Your Chase Manhattan Visa ending in 3781.

DANA: That's my husband's card. And he's at work.

CREDITOR: I'm able to take a payment from you.

DANA: I knew it. Before the test. I had a feeling. I felt different…. Like…bigger than my bones. *(She looks at the stick, then her belly. Absorbing the moment.)*

CREDITOR: *(Not really)* Ma'am. I am happy for you.

DANA: You're the first person I told!

CREDITOR: Well, I do feel special. But the purpose of my call is to collect on your past due amount. I intend to get a payment of two thousand one hundred and sixty dollars today and—

DANA: WHOA. What? Two thousand what?!

CREDITOR: And I can take that from you over the phone.

DANA: Two thousand—

CREDITOR: Two thousand one hundred and sixty dollars and zero cents.

(A long beat)

DANA: Well, that's just wrong. There's a mistake.

CREDITOR: We'd really like to settle this now.

DANA: I understand you're just doing your job—

CREDITOR: This account is three months past due and—

DANA: Excuse me. I was…I'm trying to tell you that you have to understand that my husband pays that

bill. I'm sure this is some mistake and he already
sent payment in and I wouldn't want to just give you
money without checking with him first.

CREDITOR: This account has been past due for three
months now.

DANA: I don't think so.

CREDITOR: Ninety-two days, to be exact.

DANA: No. That doesn't sound right. This is a mistake.
There's some error. We pay our bills on time.

CREDITOR: The late fees are piling up.

DANA: My husband's in between contracts right now
and things aren't as…flush…as they used to be. That's
all. But I'm sure he sent the payment in and I don't
want to double pay.

CREDITOR: I thought you said he was at work.

DANA: What?

CREDITOR: You said he was at work. Before. And just
now you said he's in between contracts.

DANA: I don't see how this is any of your business—

CREDITOR: I am sorry to hear about your husband's
unemployment—

DANA: He's just between contracts.

CREDITOR: I'd just really like to resolve this past due
amount today. We'd hate to have this go too far. You
don't want that. You're already on the naughty list—

DANA: What?!

CREDITOR: There are many people between contracts
who still manage to pay their debts, Mrs Washington.
It's called being a good American. It's about priorities.
Surely you have some savings you can use to be a
responsible adult.

DANA: Excuse me?

CREDITOR: Bad credit is a very bad thing and you people who don't pay your bills are very very bad people.

(DANA *is too stunned to respond.*)

CREDITOR: Let's, you know what, never mind what I just said. I don't know where that came from. *(Beat)* Hello?

DANA: I'M HAVING A BABY!!!

(Pause)

CREDITOR: Congratulations, Mrs Washington. We'll try this again later.

(Dial tone)

(DANA *stares at the phone.*)

(Just stands there for a beat)

(MIKE *enters in his jeans and hooded sweatshirt. Laptop bag slung over his shoulder.* DANA *turns to see him.*)

MIKE: Hey.

(MIKE *crosses to* DANA *and kisses her on the cheek. She gags.*)

MIKE: What's wrong?

DANA: You smell like…popcorn.

MIKE: That's weird. *(He flops down on the couch and grabs the remote.)*

DANA: What movie did you see?

MIKE: I didn't see a movie. I was applying to jobs.

(Off DANA*'s look:)*

MIKE: What?

DANA: I can smell the popcorn all over you.

(Beat)

MIKE: Fine. Okay. You got me. *Madagascar 2.*

DANA: *Madagascar 2?*

MIKE: The sequel to *Madagascar 1.*

DANA: The Disney movie?

MIKE: I don't know if it's Disney. Is it? It's animated.

DANA: Are you twelve?

MIKE: It was the only movie playing at eleven AM. Jesus. What the hell do you care, anyway?

DANA: You said you were applying to jobs.

MIKE: I needed to clear my head. I'll do it later.

DANA: I got a call from Chase Manhattan Visa just now.

MIKE: Okay…

DANA: Why didn't you tell me we weren't paying our Visa bill?

MIKE: You want to have this conversation now?

DANA: What's that supposed to mean?

MIKE: Just that you never want to have this conversation.

DANA: Don't make this my fault.

MIKE: Let's sit down and talk about it. Let's talk about our debt and budget and figure this out. Right now.

DANA: I resent your tone.

MIKE: I'm saying let's talk. You're reading into my tone.

DANA: No, I'm not. You blame me. It's in your tone.

MIKE: Jesus, Dana. Do you want to sit down and talk about this or not?

DANA: Three months without paying the bill and now you want to talk?

MIKE: I've been trying to talk to you, Dana. But there's always some excuse.

DANA: See! You do blame me. You blame me for this. You blame me because I was the one that wanted this house so much. Don't even try to deny it. *(Long beat)* Aren't you gonna say anything?

(MIKE doesn't say anything. DANA shoves the pregnancy test stick at him.)

(He looks at the stick. Takes him a moment to realize what it is. Then:)

MIKE: Holy shit!

(DANA turns away from MIKE.)

MIKE: Dana. Look at me. *(Beat)* Honey.

(MIKE goes to DANA. He gently takes her hand.)

MIKE: This is the most amazing news.

DANA: Is it?

MIKE: We're having a baby!

(DANA softens. MIKE touches her belly.)

MIKE: I'll find a job. It doesn't matter. I'll do whatever it takes. We'll sell the house if we have to and—

DANA: I don't want to sell the house.

MIKE: I know. We'll figure it out. Remember? We could live in a tunnel or a drop of rain or—

DANA: This is our house. This is where our baby will sleep. I don't want to sell the house.

Robbie Tries to Help the Widow Move On

(ROBBIE sits, in his jacket, in FLORENCE's living room. She—all bundled up—serves him some cocoa.)

FLORENCE: Is it warm enough? The cocoa.

ROBBIE: Yes. Hot.

FLORENCE: Nice to get something warm in your belly.

ROBBIE: Thank you. I do appreciate it.

FLORENCE: You're out there all day in that cold. It's the least I could do.

ROBBIE: I think it may be colder in here.

FLORENCE: Oh no. Don't be silly. *(Realizing something suddenly)* Darn it all.

ROBBIE: Is everything okay?

(FLORENCE gets up.)

FLORENCE: I forgot the marshmallow.

ROBBIE: No, that's okay. Don't bother…

(FLORENCE's already exiting.)

(ROBBIE sits for a beat. Then gets up and crosses to the window. Looks out)

(She returns with one marshmallow. Drops it in his mug.)

FLORENCE: There. The marshmallow makes all the difference.

ROBBIE: Thank you. You got your windows winterized at least.

FLORENCE: Oh, they've been that way for years. Martin died in the winter. He winterized them before he passed. Guess I was lucky with that. I just left them. *(Beat)* Might snow today they say.

ROBBIE: Yeah. *(Still looking out the window.)* Is that an oak tree?

FLORENCE: Chestnut.

ROBBIE: It's a beaut.

FLORENCE: Been watching it grow for thirty-eight years. It is a nice tree.

ROBBIE: Messy though. The chestnuts, I bet.

FLORENCE: It was easier before. Martin would gather them up and I'd make use of them in the kitchen.

ROBBIE: You'd roast them?

(FLORENCE *nods proudly.*)

ROBBIE: Now that's a lot of work, roasting chestnuts.

FLORENCE: Yes. But worth it. For the smell. The soul of this house smells like roasted chestnuts.

ROBBIE: Huh. Bet you won't miss the upkeep of this place. Big house for one woman without any help.

(FLORENCE *doesn't respond. Instead, crosses to the fireplace and begins to start a fire.* ROBBIE *helps her.*)

ROBBIE: You do have somewhere to go, don't you?

FLORENCE: Martin's been dead for five years now.

ROBBIE: Florence. Do you have somewhere to live?

FLORENCE: This room didn't used to be here when we bought the house. It's an addition. Did you know that? Martin built it. With his own two hands. And the neighbors' hands. A community effort. Things used to be like that.

ROBBIE: Mrs Rainwater—

FLORENCE: How's your cocoa, Robbie? Better drink it before it gets cold.

ROBBIE: Mrs Rainwater, you need to find somewhere to go. I really hope you're making plans. Because I'm gonna have to come back here and it won't be for a cup of cocoa.

FLORENCE: You used to be such a rabble rouser.

ROBBIE: I'm looking around and I don't see anything packed.

FLORENCE: The Fifth Amendment states: Nor be deprived of life, liberty or property, without due process of law—

ROBBIE: There was due process of law. You never showed up for it.

FLORENCE: I knew it'd been five years since Martin died because that's when the arm was up. Five-year arm. We owned this house free and clear for years, you know. But then I took out that loan and the arm is up.

ROBBIE: I know this is no ideal scenario and it's awkward as hell to talk about but I'm here to make sure you have a plan and from what I can see, you don't. Right or wrong, Mrs Rainwater, the bank owns your home now and you're gonna have to leave.

FLORENCE: Let's talk about something else.

ROBBIE: Mrs Rainwater. When I come back, you know what that means, right?

FLORENCE: You have a job to do.

ROBBIE: I really don't want to kick you out of your own house.

FLORENCE: Yes. Well. Don't be troubled by me. I have a plan.

ROBBIE: You do?

FLORENCE: I do.

ROBBIE: You want me to pack up some boxes?

FLORENCE: Robbie—

ROBBIE: I'm trying to help you.

FLORENCE: Then let me stay. Go. Get out. And don't come back. Pretend I'm not here. This house isn't here. We're gone and off your list. Okay? Do that. That would help me. Leave me here in peace.

ROBBIE: I could do that. But the sheriff won't. If it's not me, it'll be someone else from the sheriff's department. And trust me, you'd rather have me.

FLORENCE: Then just let me enjoy my house while I'm still here. I don't want to look around and see boxes. I just want to sit with my memories a little while longer. I don't care what name's on the deed. As long as I'm here. Living here. It's still mine… where I lived my life with Martin.

(ROBBIE considers this. Then stands)

ROBBIE: Okay. *(He heads to the door.)* Mrs Rainwater?

FLORENCE: What?

ROBBIE: I'm still making something of myself.

FLORENCE: Well you got some time left.

Woman Chooses Death Over Foreclosure

(Reporters take the stage…)

DIANE ZURICH: In one of the most extreme foreclosure-related tragedies to date, a Nevada wife and mother chose death over foreclosure. On the day the bank was to foreclose on her home, housewife Loretta Benson faxed a letter to her mortgage company that read in part—

(LORETTA BENSON enters.)

LORETTA: "By the time you foreclose on my house, I'll be dead."

DIANE ZURICH: "By the time you foreclose on my house, I'll be dead."

HUGO STORM: And then she hung herself with a dog leash.

DIANE ZURICH: It's reported that in addition to her fax to the mortgage company she also left a suicide note instructing her husband to use the insurance money to pay off the house.

LORETTA: I didn't know what else to do. I faxed the letter. Then…did it. I couldn't find any rope.

DIANE ZURICH: Apparently, Loretta's plan was to end her life before her house was auctioned that same day. And as it turned out, interested buyers arrived at the house while Loretta's body was still inside.

HUGO STORM: Sources say that Mr Benson—a mechanic—was completely unaware of their financial straits. The foreclosure of the family home came entirely as a surprise to him.

(JIM BENSON *appears.*)

JIM: Loretta handled all the finances.

LORETTA: He made the money. I paid the bills.

JIM: I had no clue. No clue.

HUGO STORM: Some viewers might find it hard to believe that such dire financial circumstances went undetected by a spouse for so long.

LORETTA: I intercepted all the letters from the mortgage company and I'd shred them before Jim got home from work.

JIM: I don't understand how this happened. This didn't happen.

DIANE ZURICH: The mortgage on the Benson home hadn't been paid in forty-two months.

HUGO STORM: That's three and a half years.

JIM: Where did all the money go?

HUGO STORM: Three and a half years!

JIM: Why didn't you come to me?

LORETTA: I put it in my note. Didn't you get my note? I was overwhelmed. I had no one to talk to.

JIM: You could have talked to me.

LORETTA: No. I couldn't. You work so hard and I...I couldn't do my one job. I couldn't bear the look in your eye.

JIM: But I have nothing without you.

LORETTA: You have the house.

(JIM *cries silent suffering tears.*)

(LORETTA *watches. Regretting*)

(JIM *and* LORETTA *exit.*)

HUGO STORM: For viewers wondering whether or not insurance companies will pay in the event of a suicide, the answer is yes.

DIANE ZURICH: Really?

HUGO STORM: As long as the policy is more than two years old.

(*Reporter is paused by the power of a DVR remote... controlled by* DANA.)

(DANA *crosses with the remote to the couch where* MIKE *is lounging.*)

(DANA *turns off the TV. Reporters disappears.*)

DANA: Want to go for a walk?

MIKE: I was watching that.

DANA: It's really nice out. We should go for a walk.

MIKE: I don't really feel like it.

DANA: What about the beach? We haven't gone to the beach in ages.

MIKE: Traffic.

DANA: Okay. Well...we could—

MIKE: I just want to watch TV and relax.

DANA: You've been watching TV for hours.

(Off MIKE's look.)

DANA: Well, you have. All you do is watch TV.

MIKE: All I do is watch TV?

DANA: Well…lately. It seems that way. Today.

MIKE: I applied to ten jobs today already.

DANA: You did?

MIKE: Yep.

DANA: Oh.

MIKE: Yeah.

DANA: I didn't know that. How could I have known that?

MIKE: I don't know, Dana.

DANA: Don't. I'm sorry.

MIKE: We never should have bought this house.

DANA: Mike.

MIKE: It was a…mistake.

DANA: Don't say that.

MIKE: We never should have bought this house.

DANA: You love this house.

MIKE: No. You love this house.

(DANA looks to MIKE for a response.)

(He takes the remote from her and turns the TV back on.)

(We hear the Simpsons theme song as we cross-fade to…)

Dana Makes an Effort

(DANA *sits in front of her house finishing a sign that reads:*
EVERYTHING MUST GO!)

(Her phone rings. CREDITOR 2 *enters wearing a headset.)*

DANA: Hello?

CREDITOR 2: Hello. Good afternoon. This is Bank of
America calling for Mrs. Washington.

DANA: I've already told you we can't pay the bill. Why
do you keep calling?

CREDITOR 2: Are you Dana Washington?

DANA: Now is not a good time.

CREDITOR 2: Yet you answered your phone.

DANA: I can't stand the constant ringing! And you
people have not been very nice. I told you about my
husband losing his job and you immediately raised our
rates. How does that help?!

CREDITOR 2: So you are Dana Washington, then.

DANA: Look. We're trying to cooperate with you. We
know we owe you money that we can't pay right now
and we want you to know that we're good people and
that we are committed to repaying this debt and we're
doing everything in our power. But right now we can't.
So…I don't know what more there is to say.

CREDITOR 2: Don't you have any relatives you can
borrow money from?

DANA: Are you serious?

CREDITOR 2: You said you were doing everything
in your power. A lot of people borrow money from
family to get out of debt.

DANA: There's no one. Okay?

CREDITOR 2: Have you even asked? I know it can be embarrassing, but if you just ask, you might be surprised to find—

DANA: I'm going to hang up now. *(She hangs up. She puts the sign on display.)*

(Phone rings again.)

DANA: Stop calling.

CREDITOR 2: Mrs Dana Washington?

DANA: Numero incorrecto. *(She disconnects again.)*

(It rings again. DANA hits ignore.)

(It rings again immediately. And again. And again. She looks at it, is about to throw it, then answers.)

DANA: No podemos pagarte! Basta con las llamadas!

DANA'S MOM: What? *(Beat)* Dana?

DANA: Mom?

DANA'S MOM: What was that all about?

DANA: Hi.

DANA'S MOM: Is everything okay?

DANA: I'm good. How are you?

DANA'S MOM: Honey, it's me. You can talk to me.

DANA: I'm having a yard sale today.

DANA'S MOM: Oh, that's great. Getting rid of stuff to make room for the baby?

DANA: Yeah.

DANA'S MOM: What are you selling?

DANA: I just sold our wedding dishes to a very nice lady who promised to take care of them.

DANA'S MOM: What?! Is that a joke? *(Beat)* Dana?

DANA: Yeah.

DANA'S MOM: Is everything okay with you and Mike?

DANA: Everything's fine.

DANA'S MOM: How's your sex life?

DANA: What?!

DANA'S MOM: Honey, it's me. We can talk about this stuff. It's important.

DANA: Oh my god. Mom. I have a lot of people here right, so I should—

DANA'S MOM: Wait! I was calling to tell you that the CIA is hiring.

DANA: The CIA?

DANA'S MOM: With your Spanish you'd be an asset to them, I think.

DANA: I have a job, Mom.

DANA'S MOM: Yes. But with no benefits and no security. But at the CIA you'd have wonderful benefits and job security.

DANA: I'm about to have a baby and you want me to work for the CIA.

DANA'S MOM: Not as a spy. Nothing dangerous. I'm just saying, it's something to look into. I hear they pay well.

DANA: Okay.

DANA'S MOM: I read this article that there are a lot of Federal government jobs opening up in Los Angeles. You'd get great health care which is important in case anything goes wrong with the baby. Not to worry you, but—

DANA: Thanks, Mom.

DANA'S MOM: I'm just trying to help.

DANA: I know.

DANA'S MOM: I'll send you the article.

DANA: Okay. I really should go.

DANA'S MOM: If you're feeling stressed about the baby that's normal. Just try to make sure you burn off the stress with exercise. I can't emphasize that enough.

DANA: I know.

DANA'S MOM: Because, I don't want to worry you, but when you're stressed, your body produces cortisol. And that is not good for the baby. But exercise can burn off cortisol. There's this article that talks about the link—

DANA: Mom. I really have to go. I'm sorry.

DANA'S MOM: Okay. You're resilient. You always have been. So don't worry.

DANA: Okay.

DANA'S MOM: Dana…

DANA: Yeah?

DANA'S MOM: *(After a long beat)* Maybe I should come out there now. Before the baby's born.

DANA: I'm fine, Mom. Really. Let's just keep the plan as is. Okay?

DANA'S MOM: Okay. Just take care of yourself.

DANA: I will. I am. I love you.

DANA'S MOM: I love you.

(DANA *and* DANA'S MOM *disconnect.*)

(MIKE *enters.*)

(DANA *looks at* MIKE.)

DANA: What's wrong?

(MIKE *hands* DANA *a piece of paper.*)

DANA: What's this? *(Looking at it)* When did this come?! *(Beat)* What does this mean? They said we had options!

MIKE: We do have an option. One option. I made an appointment to meet with the Realtor today. *(Beat)* It's just a house. *(Beat)* The Realtor will be here at three.

DANA: The CIA is hiring! Mom wants me to apply. If I got a job there, then maybe—

MIKE: It's too late for any of that.

DANA: You don't know how this is gonna go.

MIKE: I know how it will go if we do nothing. You want to be surprised one day by someone from the Sheriff's department tossing us out on the street? *(Beat)* I know you don't want to sell the house, but—

DANA: Okay, just…

MIKE: If we can sell it now, we might have a chance and/

DANA: Okay/

MIKE: …the Realtor thinks she might already have a buyer for the house.

DANA: Mike. I said okay.

MIKE: Okay?

DANA: We'll meet with the Realtor.

MIKE: Okay. Good. *(Beat)* Thank you.

(MIKE exits. DANA goes back to her sign and writes the words "EXCEPT US" after "EVERYTHING MUST GO.")

(She sets the sign up.)

(Lights)

END OF ACT ONE

ACT TWO

Woman in Chains Fights Eviction

(Reporters again.)

DIANE ZURICH: Jenny Lancaster, her husband and their four dogs have lived in their Orlando home for nearly twenty years. Now, they are being evicted…

HUGO STORM: …but Jenny Lancaster is not having it. She's defying eviction by chaining herself to her home.

DIANE ZURICH: Ms Lancaster said she will remain chained to her home until—

JENNY LANCASTER *appears—chained to her house.)*

JENNY LANCASTER: I will remain chained to MY home until the Florida State Legislature elected officials respond to these massive evictions and foreclosures that are going on in our county. It's utterly wrong.

DIANE ZURICH: Lancaster recently lost her job and the couple's salary was cut in half. They have an adjustable rate mortgage—

HUGO STORM: Also known as an "ARM".

DIANE ZURICH: And can't afford the four-thousand-nine-hundred-and-fifty dollar monthly payments.

HUGO STORM: So instead of taking responsibility for her debts, she is hoping that a Home Depot chain and pad lock will serve as her own personal bailout?

JENNY LANCASTER: I will not allow them to take this home from us!

DIANE ZURICH: How the Lancasters ended up in this position is part of a larger story about the housing crisis.

HUGO STORM: Ms Lancaster describes herself as a victim—

JENNY LANCASTER: I was a target by the mortgage companies. The banks peddling easy credit. Feeding like blood-thirsty vampires on average, hard-working Americans. Sucking us dry.

HUGO STORM: However she has declared bankruptcy several times—

JENNY LANCASTER: That ain't got nothin' to do with any of this! Besides, plenty of business people declare bankruptcy.

HUGO STORM: In 2000 Ms Lancaster's second husband had the house paid off completely. Then one night in a domestic outburst following a few too many glasses of Franzia, she took a Louisville Slugger to his head.

DIANE ZURICH: Really?

JENNY LANCASTER: Okay, I don't know where you're getting your facts. I think you need a new fact checker. Because I don't drink. And he told me to swing that baseball bat at him. He egged me on. Begged me to do it.

HUGO STORM: She kept the house in the divorce and proceeded to use it like an ATM. This little act here? Chaining herself to her house? She's nothing but an attention hungry scavenger.

JENNY LANCASTER: I had to do this. No one would listen to me! No one! This is not fair! You can't just say whatever you want about people. You're supposed to be unbiased. You think you know me?!

DIANE ZURICH: Jenny Lancaster: a victim of the mortgage crisis and immoral blood-thirsty lenders?

HUGO STORM: Or an attention-hungry parasitic whore? You decide.

Dana Washington Builds a Nest

(DANA *enters with painting supplies—a roller, a gallon of mint green paint, a pan and painting coveralls.*)

DANA: Dear President Barack Obama… (*She sets the supplies down. She picks up the coveralls and begins to put them on over her clothes.*)

ENSEMBLE 1: Dear President Barack Obama…

ENSEMBLE 2: Dear President Obama…

ENSEMBLE 3: Dear Mr President…

DANA: I voted for you.

ENSEMBLE 1: I voted for you.

ENSEMBLE 2: I voted for you.

ENSEMBLE 3: I did not vote for you.

DANA: I campaigned for you. Door to door. In hundred degree temperatures in the desert.

ENSEMBLE 1: I got my whole family to vote for you.

ENSEMBLE 2: I have a HOPE bumper sticker.

ENSEMBLE 3: I still can't believe you were elected.

(DANA *pours some paint into the pan, dips the roller into the paint and puts it to the wall.*)

DANA: I'm a homeowner.

ENSEMBLE 1: I'm a homeowner.

ENSEMBLE 2: I'm a homeowner.

ENSEMBLE 3: I'm a proud homeowner. Have been since the Reagan administration.

DANA: That's why I'm writing.

ENSEMBLE 1: I'm writing to ask…

DANA: …to beg…

ENSEMBLE 1: …for your help.

ENSEMBLE 2: I'm writing because I don't know what else to do.

ENSEMBLE 3: I'm writing to give you a piece of my mind.

DANA: We've missed a few mortgage payments and now…

ENSEMBLE 1: We're in foreclosure.

ENSEMBLE 2: We're fighting to keep our home out of foreclosure.

ENSEMBLE 3: House was paid off during W's first term. Decided to remodel. Borrowed from the equity in our house and then…shit hit the fan.

DANA: We've been trying to work with Countrywide—

ENSEMBLE 1: Wells Fargo—

ENSEMBLE 2: Bank of America—

ENSEMBLE 3: Bank of America. What a joke.

DANA: We tried to renegotiate our loan. We were hoping for a loan modification.

ENSEMBLE 1: A modification would help us.

ENSEMBLE 2: If only they would have gotten back to us.

ENSEMBLE 3: If only they didn't keep losing our paperwork.

DANA: And then you announced your Home Affordable Modification Program…

ENSEMBLE 1: Hamp.

ENSEMBLE 2: Hamp.

ENSEMBLE 3: Hamp. What a joke.

DANA: We were told it was too soon. No one knows anything about it. Did you know that? The banks have no idea how to implement this program. I thought you should know that.

ENSEMBLE 1: We wrote letters of hardship.

ENSEMBLE 2: We jumped through all the banks' hoops.

ENSEMBLE 3: This is how every day hard working Americans are treated in your administration? What happened to HOPE? Been unemployed now for six months.

DANA: We keep applying for jobs.

ENSEMBLE 1: I apply to at least five jobs a day.

ENSEMBLE 2: Does applying to jobs even work anymore?

ENSEMBLE 3: What did you do with all the jobs?!

DANA: I even applied to the CIA. Maybe you could put in a good word for me.

ENSEMBLE 1: The banks got bailed out. I don't mean to be bitter, but what about us?

ENSEMBLE 2: What's gonna happen to us?

ENSEMBLE 3: Where's our bailout?

DANA: I'm writing you, Mr President…

ENSEMBLE 1: Mr President…

ENSEMBLE 2: Mr President…

ENSEMBLE 3: Mr President…

DANA: Because we're about to lose everything and I just don't know what else to do.

ENSEMBLE 1: I don't what else to do.

ENSEMBLE 2: Is there something we can do?

ENSEMBLE 3: I'll tell you what you need to do.

DANA: I'm sorry. I feel silly even writing, but you seem so approachable. Like you actually read the mail you receive. Like you'll read this letter and you'll want to help.

ENSEMBLE 3: You can stop these foreclosures and start investigating the real criminals- the bankers.

ENSEMBLE 1: I know you want to help.

ENSEMBLE 2: It's not an easy situation, but…

ENSEMBLE 3: You say you're about change? Prove it.

ENSEMBLE 2: I do believe you want to help us. You would if you could, right?

DANA: I believe that you're on our side.

ENSEMBLE 1: You want to keep us in our homes.

ENSEMBLE 2: But you can't, can you?

ENSEMBLE 3: You could help if you really wanted to. You're the President of the United States of America. You could help.

DANA: So, please. Help us.

ENSEMBLE 1: I just wish…

ENSEMBLE 2: I wish…

ENSEMBLE 3: If wishes were red state votes, you wouldn't be president.

DANA: Sometimes I feel like a mama bird building my nest. Michelle probably did that, right? Nested? I'm a mama bird building my nest. It's what I'm supposed to be doing.

ENSEMBLE 1: This is more than a house. It's our home.

ENSEMBLE 2: It's our nest egg.

ENSEMBLE 3: It's our safe place.

DANA: And I refuse to give up on our home. As long as we're here, it's ours. I have hope that something will materialize.

ENSEMBLE 1: I still hope.

ENSEMBLE 2: I'm afraid I'm losing hope.

ENSEMBLE 3: I'm afraid this will only get worse.

DANA: I believe in you, Mr President. I believe you will help us through this. I believe in the power of positivity. *(She dips the roller and puts it to the wall again.)* I believe in painting my baby's room.

(MIKE enters. ENSEMBLE exits the scene.)

(A beat as MIKE takes in the scene.)

MIKE: Honey?

DANA: Before you say anything, mint green is neutral. Works for boy or girl. I think it's soothing.

(MIKE gently takes the roller from DANA's hand.)

DANA: Give it back, Mike. I'm not done.

MIKE: Why are you doing this?

DANA: Just give me the brush.

MIKE: Dana—

DANA: Charcoal is not a happy color. Charcoal won't do for our baby's room. Mint green is neutral and soothing.

(The phone rings. DANA and MIKE ignore it.)

(She takes the paint roller back [he lets her] and continues.)

(He watches. Then)

MIKE: You remember painting our bedroom in the apartment? We were too lazy to move the furniture.

DANA: You were too lazy to move the furniture.

MIKE: Well. It took us twice as long. Trying to paint around everything. And then having to remove the paint from where we spilled. *(He laughs.)* You had an itch on your face and used the paint roller to scratch it. Blue paint all over your face.

DANA: And then you kissed me and got it all over your face.

MIKE: You looked so cute. I couldn't resist.

(DANA and MIKE share a laugh. Then she dips the roller in the paint and puts it to the wall again.)

MIKE: Dana, it makes no sense to paint this room.

DANA: You just don't want to help me.

MIKE: Baby, you're painting for somebody else. This room doesn't exist for us anymore. This isn't the baby's room. It's the bank's. It's the bank's room. These are the bank's walls, the bank's windows, the bank's paint—

DANA: I paid cash for this paint. We just won't pay the cable bill.

MIKE: We haven't paid the cable bill in months. Or our student loan bills or the credit card bills.

DANA: There's a solution for everything. Things we can do without.

MIKE: There's only moving on. Starting again.

DANA: This paint goes on so nicely.

MIKE: We fucked up. And we don't live here anymore.

Dana doesn't say anything. Then.

DANA: You should go for a walk. It would do you some good. Cheer you up.

MIKE: A walk?

DANA: Yes. Or a run. Endorphins. You know. I'm really loving this paint.

MIKE: This can't be fixed by jogging.

DANA: Well it can't be fixed by not jogging. Just...be positive. You have to be positive. Go for a walk or a jog and be...positive. Your negativity does not help, you know. And I'm not going to pay attention to it anymore.

MIKE: I'm not being negative. I'm being realistic. Dealing with reality. Real life. Actuality. Actual things that exist. Our circumstances and the facts. Such as the fact that we have negative forty-seven dollars in our checking account and you don't get paid for another week. Another fact. We have twenty-three voicemail messages from creditors and I have zero fucking job prospects.

DANA: I found a crib on Freecycle today. It's free. And they only used it for one baby so it's in pretty good condition. I'm still looking for the perfect glider. I don't know if I want just an old fashioned rocking chair or a glider. I'm leaning towards a rocker. I like tradition.

(DANA *paints.* MIKE *just watches, unable to reach her.*)

Florence Rainwater Becomes Immortal

(FLORENCE *sits in her armchair, bundled up...waiting for what's coming.*)

(*Doorbell rings and rings.*)

(FLORENCE *doesn't move.*)

(*Pounding on the door*)

ROBBIE: *(OS)* Florence! I know you're in there. You have to come out and let us do our job.

(No response from FLORENCE.*)*

ROBBIE: *(OS)* Mrs Rainwater! Please just open up. I promise to take care of you. It's time to vacate. Today's the day. Time's up. I'm sorry. You know I am.

(More pounding)

ROBBIE: Open up, now. I don't want to have to do this, but we'll have to bust the door down. We have a warrant this time.

(Ramming against the door)

*(*FLORENCE *slowly stands and crosses to the other side of the room to the hall closet [or cabinet] and removes a shotgun.)*

*(*ROBBIE *looking through the window sees this.)*

ROBBIE: *(Frantic)* FLORENCE!!!

*(*FLORENCE *carries the shotgun to her bedroom.)*

(Another shuddering ram against the door.)

*(*FLORENCE *exits to the bedroom.)*

(A third ramming against the door and ROBBIE *busts through.)*

(A gun shot from the bedroom)

The Disappearance of Mike Washington

(Lights up on MIKE.*)*

(He addresses the audience.)

MIKE: I keep thinking about Tetris. You know that falling puzzle piece video game? The puzzle pieces are different sizes and colors and they fall from the top of the screen. The object is to guide the Tetris pieces into place as they fall in order to make solid rows all

the way across the game board. Without any spaces.
You're supposed to get them to fit perfectly together
and when you do, they disappear…making room for
the pieces that continue to fall. The pieces never stop
falling. They keep coming. Slow at first.

(Unpaid bills fall from the sky. Slow at first)

MIKE: And you can manage that pace. You're doing
all right. And you start to feel good about it. Auto-
pilot kicks in. Just when you're getting cocky, they fall
faster.

(The bills fall faster.)

MIKE: And you make your first mistake. Then you
adjust. And you're back on track. Fitting the pieces.
Turning them ninety degrees, getting them to fit just
right. Your confidence builds. You're agile. Good
reflexes. Keeping up with the game.
Then they fall faster. And it's not so easy any more.
You up your game. Your pace quickens. Muscles
tighten. Stomach twists. They fall faster and faster. And
the faster they fall, the more flustered you get. Your
heart races. Palms sweat.

*(MIKE's heart races. His palms sweat. He looks up at the
bills that continue to fall on him.)*

MIKE: The game is faster than you. Without a doubt.
Too fast. I can't keep up. The pieces will pile up. Pile
up. Pile up. One on top of the other, filling the screen.
No more room. But they keep coming. Failure is
imminent.
I knew how to win. You just keep up. Stay calm. But I
got too flustered. Made too many mistakes. And now
it's too late. I'm out of room and about to fail. With
Tetris though, there's always the end. Game over.
Where everything just stops.

(The bills stop. All is silent for a beat.)

(MIKE *breathes.*)

MIKE: And you can start again if you want. That's the beauty of it. You press play and you get a new screen. Blank. Room for all the pieces to fit. You can avoid the mistakes you made the last time. Keep your cool a little bit longer. Learn some tricks to make them fit.
Life is like Tetris except the pieces never stop falling…

(*The bills continue to bury him alive.*)

MIKE: And there's no such thing as a blank screen. I keep looking, but for the life of me I can't fucking find the start button.

(*Bills stop. Lights go out just before* MIKE's *buried alive.*)

(*Lights flick on again.* DANA *enters. Walks through the metaphoric pile of bills…ignoring them.*)

DANA: Mike?? (*She looks. Listens. Nothing. Again*) Mike.

(*More listening. Looking.* DANA *doesn't see* MIKE, *though he's standing right there seeing her.*)

DANA: I thought I heard… Nothing. Guess I'm hearing things. (*To her belly*) Sorry for waking you, baby. Let's go back to bed. Shhhh… It's okay.

The Resurrection of Florence Rainwater

(DIANE ZURICH *and* HUGO STORM *interview* FLORENCE— *who is lying in a hospital bed.*)

(*An ECG beeps in the background. [Sound effect might be provided by the* ENSEMBLE.*])*

DIANE ZURICH: Mrs Rainwater? May I call you Florence? Such a nice name.

HUGO STORM: Florence Nightingale.

DIANE ZURICH: Florence, why did you do it? (*No response*) Mrs Rainwater?

FLORENCE: Why did I do it? Why did I do what?

DIANE ZURICH: Why did you leverage your house after it was paid off?

HUGO STORM: Was it for drugs?

DIANE ZURICH: Let me rephrase. What drove you to suicide?

HUGO STORM: Let me rephrase. Why a shotgun? *(No response)* Why a shotgun? Mrs Rainwater?

DIANE ZURICH: Florence.

HUGO STORM: Florence. Why a shotgun?

FLORENCE: It's all I had.

DIANE ZURICH: Do you think if you had used a revolver you would have been successful?

FLORENCE: What do you mean?

DIANE ZURICH: A revolver is smaller.

HUGO STORM: A handgun. More compact.

DIANE ZURICH: Easier to wield. More…

HUGO STORM: …precise.

FLORENCE: I didn't have a revolver. I had a shotgun.

DIANE ZURICH: Your husband's shotgun.

FLORENCE: Martin's gun. Yes.

HUGO STORM: How do you think Martin would feel to know you used his shotgun to blow your head off?

FLORENCE: Martin's dead.

DIANE ZURICH: Let me rephrase. To attempt to blow your head off…

FLORENCE: It wasn't my head.

HUGO STORM: …and miss so completely.

FLORENCE: It was my heart. I was aiming for my heart.

HUGO STORM: *(After a beat)* Well, you missed that too.

(FLORENCE feels her heart.)

DIANE ZURICH: Do you ever think that maybe none of this would have happened if you had just opened your mail? Do you ever wonder about that? If you had just read the fine print?

FLORENCE: You can't stop a bull mid-charge.

HUGO STORM: Or answered your phone?

(The phone rings, filling the theatre.)

DIANE ZURICH: Go ahead.

HUGO STORM: It's about time you answer.

FLORENCE: I don't know how.

DIANE ZURICH: Again, and not to belabor the point, but...do you think that things might have been different if you had only answered—

FLORENCE: It was Martin's shotgun. It was for protection he always said. I didn't want it in the house. When he died I kept it. Because it was him. Protecting me.

(The phone stops ringing. FLORENCE appears relieved.)

(The pace quickens. As does the heart monitor.)

HUGO STORM: Was it painful?

DIANE ZURICH: Was it painful?

FLORENCE: No. Yes. I don't remember.

HUGO STORM: Have you ever tried to blow your heart out before or was this your first attempt?

DIANE ZURICH: Does suicide run in your family?

HUGO STORM: Will you try to kill yourself again?

DIANE ZURICH: Will you ever roast chestnuts again?

HUGO STORM: Have you been praying to live?

DIANE ZURICH: Have you been reading the Bible? Do
you mind if I read to you now? *(She reads to her)*
The faithful have disappeared from the land,
And there is no one left who
Is upright;
They all lie in wait for blood,
And they hunt each other
With nets.

*(ROBBIE enters reading from the Bible. He and REPORTER 1
overlap for a few lines.)*

*(As they read, FLORENCE drifts off to sleep…the ECG
slows.)*

REPORTER 1:
The best of them is like a brier,
The most upright of them a thorn hedge.
The day of their sentinels, of
Their punishment,
Has come…

ROBBIE: *(As they read, FLORENCE drifts off to sleep…the
ECG slows)*
The best of them is like a brier,
The most upright of them a thorn hedge.
The day of their sentinels, of
Their punishment,
Has come…

(Reporters exit.)

ROBBIE: *(To FLORENCE)* Real uplifting, huh. Let me
see… *(He skips ahead. Then reads)*
Put no trust in a friend
Have no confidence in a loved one;
(To FLORENCE) Now, see I just disagree. How does that
help? Who wrote this?

(FLORENCE awakens with a gasp.)

(She sits up, scaring ROBBIE *who is stunned, just looking at her.)*

(She instinctively grabs her heart.)

(Filled with pain and despair, she realizes...)

FLORENCE: I missed.

Marcus Jones Confronts the Preacher

*(*PREACHER PAULA *sits at her laptop.* MARCUS *enters.)*

PREACHER PAULA: *(Calling off)* Matthew!

MARCUS: Pastor...

PREACHER PAULA: Marcus, What a surprise.

MARCUS: I've left you messages.

PREACHER PAULA: Have you?

MARCUS: Oh you know I have. Been trying to reach you for weeks now.

PREACHER PAULA: I am just about to head out to a meeting—

MARCUS: I just need one minute of your—

PREACHER PAULA: If you talk to Matthew— *(Calling off)* Matthew! *(To* MARCUS*)* He can set something up—

MARCUS: I've been trying to get a meeting with you.

PREACHER PAULA: I understand, but this isn't a good time. Matthew can schedule—

MARCUS: I've tried that.

PREACHER PAULA: Just talk to Matthew. I'm a wreck when it comes to scheduling—

MARCUS: I'm here now and I only ask for just one minute. Please. I beg you. Please.

(Beat. PREACHER PAULA *nods.)*

MARCUS: You said that God wanted me to prosper. You said that He didn't want me to suffer anymore. (*A beat*) Was it all just bullshit?

PREACHER PAULA: Excuse me?

MARCUS: A con?

PREACHER PAULA: I resent that.

MARCUS: I have been giving to your ministry since you first started preaching in that gymnasium. I think I've earned your indulgence.

PREACHER PAULA: You're angry.

MARCUS: Damn right, I'm angry!

PREACHER PAULA: I understand your pain, Marcus. I do.

MARCUS: No you don't. No you do not understand my pain. We got that house. Hallelujah. And then you know what happened? Same day we closed on the house, I lost my day job. Same damn day. Is that a coincidence or is that God? Been trying to piece together some carpentry gigs here and there, but the money's just dried up for that sort of thing. I put everything I had just to get the house. I got no safety net. And I been out of work for months. Yesterday my car broke down. No fixing that.

PREACHER PAULA: I understand—

MARCUS: I'm wearing thrift store hand me-downs wondering how I'm going to feed my kids tonight and you stand there in front of me in a fancy suit, diamond earrings and a Rolex on your wrist and have the nerve to tell me that you understand my pain?

PREACHER PAULA: You know me, Marcus. I was once just like you. Broken. Barren. Destitute—

MARCUS: Just stop. I've been listening to you for too long. It's your turn to listen to me. I'm losing

everything because I believed you when you told me
that God wanted me to have it all. That my faith alone
would get me there. I've been faithful. I kept giving to
the ministry even when things were scarce. But all I've
known is scarcity.

PREACHER PAULA: You're just in a tight place, Marcus.
This is when you need to trust the most. Rely on your
faith right now. You're at a crossroads and you have
a choice. You can either choose to trust your future to
God or you can choose to play the victim card. Which
is it gonna be? What are you going to choose, Marcus?

MARCUS: You never turn it off, do you? You used to be
a person. An actual person. Now you're just a plastic
shell.

(A beat)

PREACHER PAULA: Why are you here?

MARCUS: That loan officer you sent my way. Came
through for us just like you said he would. You know
what he calls himself? Mr Dream Weaver. Mr Dream
Weaver. We got that house thanks to you.

PREACHER PAULA: Divine intervention.

MARCUS: Subprime.

(Beat. Beat)

PREACHER PAULA: What is it you want from me?

MARCUS: I want you to explain it to me. How this is
happening when we did everything you said. Because
it's not just me. It's scorched earth out there pastor.
More and more homeless gettin created by the day. It
ain't just me. Your whole ministry is in pain while you
sit up here—

PREACHER PAULA: Don't you think I know that? I see
that! But nothing I say will make it right.

MARCUS: You're damn right about that. *(Beat)* "In prosperity one can easily forget God." You remember that? Remember saying that?

PREACHER PAULA: You accusing me of something, Marcus?

MARCUS: "Be careful, Marcus," you said one day a long time ago when I was dreaming up a better life. "In prosperity one can easily forget God." *(Beat)* That what happened to you?

PREACHER PAULA: I'm gonna forgive your disrespect because I know you just need some place to put that anger. And I'm willing to take it. It's okay.

MARCUS: I don't need your permission.

PREACHER PAULA: I wish I could make things right for you. I do.

MARCUS: I wish you wouldn't made me believe. I actually believed. I believed I deserved it. I believed the struggle was over. I believed. *(Beat)* I wish I never had.

PREACHER PAULA: Careful, Marcus. That anger leaves no room for the Lord.

MARCUS: How did I not see it sooner? *(He takes his eraser out of his pocket and sets it down on her desk. He exits.)*

PREACHER PAULA: *(Calling after him)* I'm still a person, Marcus!

MARCUS: *(As he's exiting)* Then prove it.

Yes, I Still Live Here!

(DANA is on the phone in her robe pacing nervously.)

DANA: *(On the phone)* I can't. I can't just sit here. But I can't leave either because what if he comes back and

I'm not here. Please just drive around to some places for me, Greg, can you do that? Because you're his friend... Because it's been five hours. Because I have a feeling. I have a very bad feeling. Because I know him. I know him, Greg. I know him. And I can't help it. I'm pregnant and—DON'T you dare tell me to stop being emotional—are you kidding me?! My husband is missing and—

She takes a very deep breath and lets it out slowly. She suddenly hears something and looks towards the front door. We hear keys jingling.

DANA: *(Calling out)* Mike?! *(Into phone)* I gotta go!

(DANA *rushes towards the front door expecting to find* MIKE *and instead discovers three strangers. Door opening. Voices)*

DANA: Hello?!

(DANA *is suddenly face to face with three strangers-* REALTOR *and two* BUYERS.)

REALTOR: Oh, hello. I didn't realize—

DANA: Don't come any closer! Who are you?!

REALTOR: I'm so sorry. We didn't expect anyone to be here. *(Handing over his business card)* Lee Jones, Quick Sell Real Estate. *(Beat)* And these are my clients.

BUYER 1: Hi, I'm Dana.

BUYER 2: I'm Matt.

(BUYERS *shake* DANA's *hand enthusiastically.)*

DANA: Matt and...

BUYER 1: Dana. You have a beautiful home.

REALTOR: Do you still live here?

DANA: What? Yes. This is my home. I still live here.

BUYER 1: Should we take our shoes off?

REALTOR: No. It's fine. Why don't you go ahead and have a look around and we'll sort this out.

(The BUYERS *explore the house.)*

DANA: No!

*(*REALTOR *gently pulls* DANA *aside. She yanks her arm away.)*

DANA: You can't be here. You can't just—

REALTOR: *(To* DANA*)* I left messages with your agent.

DANA: You left messages?

REALTOR: To set up the appointment.

(Something suddenly catches BUYER 1's *eye. She is seeing the house for the first time...and it is love at first sight.)*

BUYER 1: Oh, wow. Oh my god. Look at this view! Honey!

(The BUYERS *rush towards the view and take it in hand in hand.)*

DANA: *(To* REALTOR*)* I'm not dressed.

REALTOR: We won't be long. We'll stay out of your way.

DANA: I'm in the middle of something and I wasn't expecting you otherwise I'd be dressed and I—

REALTOR: We're already here. It will only take a minute.

*(*DANA *grabs the phone and dials.)*

DANA: I'm calling my husband.

BUYER 1: Matt, the fireplace!

DANA: *(Into phone)* Mike? Mike, it's me. Again.

BUYER 2: Oooh, fireplace! Awesome!

DANA: *(Into phone)* These people just walked into our house while I was in my bathrobe and they won't leave.

BUYER 1: Vaulted ceilings…

DANA: *(Into phone)* You better come back. Now.

BUYER 2: Vaulted ceilings!

REALTOR: *(To* DANA*)* They seem to really like it.

(The BUYERS *wander the whole house.* DANA *watches protectively as they go in and out of rooms.)*

BUYER 2: *(From the bathroom)* Dana!

DANA: Yeah?

BUYER 1: Yeah?

DANA: *(Off* REALTOR'*s look)* I'm Dana. My name. That's my name…also.

BUYER 2: There's even a view from the bathroom!

*(*BUYER 1 *rushes to look.)*

REALTOR: I think it's fate.

DANA: What's fate?

REALTOR: That you have the same name. Maybe it's fate. They seem to really like the house.

DANA: You're trespassing.

REALTOR: Excuse me?

DANA: You just barged in here. I'm not even dressed.

BUYER 1: *(From the kitchen)* Oh my god, honey, they have a Viking!

REALTOR: *(To* DANA*)* Are appliances included?

DANA: I want you to leave. Please. Please leave.

BUYER 2: *(Regarding the view)* I don't like that, though.

BUYER 1: What?

BUYER 2: The telephone lines. They're pretty close to the house.

BUYER 1: They don't seem that close.

DANA: They're dangerously close. We've always hated that.

REALTOR: *(Separating from DANA)* You can always bury those. It's not too complicated.

DANA: It's really complicated, actually. We tried. My husband tried because he's always, always hated those telephone lines.

REALTOR: I've had plenty of clients get their lines buried. Just takes a phone call to the city.

DANA looks down at their feet. At their shoes. Phone rings again.

DANA: *(Answering the phone)* Mike?! *(Into phone)* Wrong number. *(She disconnects.)*

(BUYER 2 wanders into the baby's room.)

BUYER 2: Dana! Honey…this room's already set up for a baby. It's ready to go.

BUYER 1: Oh my god, it's like fate!

DANA: I need you to leave now.

REALTOR: We won't inconvenience you for much longer.

DANA: *(To REALTOR)* You shouldn't just walk into people's homes tracking in dirt and germs and bacteria and God knows what else.

REALTOR: Ma'am. I'm sorry, but this is what happens when you put your house on the market. You need to get a hold of yourself.

DANA: Oh, I need to get a hold of myself? I don't think so. I think you…you need to get out. Get out. GET THE FUCK OUT!!!

(A beat)

REALTOR: We need to move on to the next appointment. Lots of houses to see.

BUYER 1: *(To* DANA*)* Are you okay?

BUYER 2: Honey.

BUYER 1: Why are you moving? *(Immediately regrets asking)* I'm sorry.

*(*REALTOR *rushes the* BUYERS *to the door.* REALTOR *and* BUYER 2 *exit.* BUYER 1 *stops just before exiting. She turns and looks at* DANA. *She doesn't say anything, just looks at* DANA *who slowly makes eye contact.)*

BUYER 1: Are you sure you're okay?

BUYER 2: *(OS)* Dana!

*(*BUYER 1 *looks at* DANA *one last time, then exits.* DANA *finally exhales.)*

(Beat. She feels a kick from the baby.)

DANA: *(To her belly)* It's okay. Everything's gonna be okay. He's okay. Daddy's okay. He's okay he's okay he's okay.

(Knocking at the door)

DANA: *(Regarding the knocking)* No. No. Go away! Please!

DANA'S MOM: *(OS)* Hello-o? Anyone home? *(She enters.)* Dana?

DANA: Mom?!

DANA'S MOM: What's going on? You're selling the house?

*(*DANA *rushes to her and embraces her, surprising her mom by the desperation. Her baby needs her.)*

DANA'S MOM: It's okay. Everything's gonna be all right. Mommy's here now.

Mike's Life Flashes Before His Eyes

(MIKE *enters opposite and crosses downstage to the very edge of the stage. He looks out. Then down*)

MIKE: Never look down.

(MIKE *looks up. Then out. Reporter enters.*)

DIANE ZURICH: Our viewers want to know why.

HUGO STORM: Why, Mike?

DIANE ZURICH: Why are you doing this?

(*No response*)

DIANE ZURICH: Mike Washington grew up in a trailer park surrounded by cornfields in a small town in Iowa.

HUGO STORM: "If you build it, he will come."

DIANE ZURICH: Like many Americans, he worked his way from nothing in pursuit of the American Dream.

HUGO STORM: Mike worked hard to put himself through college— Working for companies such as Subway Sandwich, United Postal Service and Farm & Egg.

DIANE ZURICH: He's been a detasseler, a paper boy…

HUGO STORM: …a chicken coop cleaner…

DIANE ZURICH: …a sandwich artist, a UPS delivery man, a bar back…

HUGO STORM: …a fertilizer salesman…

DIANE ZURICH: …and finally a computer programmer. His first job out of college took him out of the state of Iowa to a life in Los Angeles he'd only imagined…

HUGO STORM: …where money came easy and spending it came easier.

DIANE ZURICH: On his way to owning a BMW, marriage and home ownership.

HUGO STORM: The American Dream.

DIANE ZURICH: *(To* HUGO STORM*)* What was he trying to prove?

(No response. Beat. Then…)

DIANE ZURICH: Dana Washington was born a Leo on a cloudy night…

HUGO STORM: …after three days of labor—

DIANE ZURICH: Really?

HUGO STORM: Mike noticed her laugh first.

MIKE: Stop.

HUGO STORM: Her free-spirited laugh that danced inside his heart.

MIKE: Stop! Do not talk about her!

DIANE ZURICH: The first time he showered at her apartment, he took a moment to picture himself as her husband.

MIKE: Shut up!

HUGO STORM: This was only their fifth date.

MIKE: Shut up! Shut up! Shut up!

DIANE ZURICH: They were on their way. The American Dream… A marriage, a BMW, a house on a hill… A baby. A dream.

HUGO STORM: The American Dream…so hard to acquire, so easy to lose.

DIANE ZURICH: Just like that it began to crumble. The dream quickly turned into… a nightmare.

MIKE: All right!!!

DIANE ZURICH: All right?

(A Beat. Silence)

HUGO STORM: What will you miss the most?

(Beat)

MIKE: *(To himself)* Meeting him.

DIANE ZURICH: Him? Your son, you mean.

(No response)

DIANE ZURICH: What are you going to do next?

MIKE: *(A beat)* Jump. *(He looks down.)*

DIANE ZURICH: Mike Washington is standing on the Colorado Street Bridge spanning the Arroyo Seco—

HUGO STORM: *(Correcting her pronunciation)* Say-co.

DIANE ZURICH: Seh-co?

HUGO STORM: SAY-co. SAY-co. Arroyo SAY-co.

DIANE ZURICH: Between Eagle Rock and Pasadena.

HUGO STORM: Built in 1913, this historic bridge with its Beaux Arts arches came to be known as "Suicide Bridge" during the Great Depression—

MIKE: They'll be better off without me. Sure, they'll miss me. She'll be sad. It'll be hard, but they'll be free from my debts. My failure. And eventually they'll move on.

DIANE ZURICH: She is resilient. Your wife.

(MIKE just looks at reporter.)

HUGO STORM: What else?

MIKE: I'm a pathetic excuse for a human being.

DIANE ZURICH: What else?

MIKE: It's all my fault and I deserve to die.

HUGO STORM: Hmm.

MIKE: I can't live with my failure one second more!

HUGO STORM: Of course it's really just about you. Suicide is…

MIKE: The only logical answer.

REPORTER 2: …the most selfish act imaginable.

DIANE ZURICH: You made a mistake. You can start over. People do it all the time.

HUGO STORM: All the time.

MIKE: That's…no. Not the point.

DIANE ZURICH: Because it would require you to live with your failure one second more?

HUGO STORM: You'd have to man up?

MIKE: I didn't ask for any of this!!!!

DIANE ZURICH: My husband didn't ask for colon cancer. And I didn't ask for him to die. But you go on.

MIKE: If you'd just let me explain—

HUGO STORM: I'm outta here. I have another story.

DIANE ZURICH: Really?

(Reporters leave.)

(Beat)

(MIKE takes one step back.)

MIKE: Fuck.

Dana Has a Moment

(DANA sits in the rocker. MOM enters with two mugs. She hands DANA one.)

DANA'S MOM: Ginger tea. Good for nausea.

(Beat)

DANA: It's all my fault.

DANA'S MOM: I'm sure that's not true. How is it all your fault?

DANA: I had to have this house. And he knew it was too much. I thought it was a risk but one we had to take. And then the bank gave us all this money and… We took it. *(Beat)* It's my fault. And now Mike's…and I'm so worried.

DANA'S MOM: He's fine, honey.

DANA: How do you know that? You don't know that. He hasn't been himself. He's depressed. I didn't realize how depressed. But…it weighs on him. Not being able to find a job. And…when I woke up in the middle of the night to pee and he wasn't there, I knew.

DANA'S MOM: What did you know?

DANA: That something is not right. He never does this. He never just turns off his phone like this.

DANA'S MOM: Maybe the battery died.

DANA: Where is he?!

DANA'S MOM: He could just be…I don't know. Could there be, I don't want to say it but, another…another woman?

DANA: There's no other woman!

DANA'S MOM: Okay.

(DANA's pacing.)

(The following should overlap)

DANA'S MOM: Honey, you should sit and try to relax.

DANA: My heart is like squeezing itself and I'm…I feel like I'm underwater or something like I'm…in a nightmare and the air is too thick to breathe and—

DANA'S MOM: Breathe, honey. Breathe.

DANA: What would I do without him? What what? I can't. He's been so down and I've been just so hard on him and…and…like living in my own little bubble where everything's fine…but really this could all go away all of it and I wouldn't care because I just want Mike. That's all I want. I just want Mike.

DANA'S MOM: The stress isn't good for—

DANA: I'm gonna go look for him. You stay here and wait in case he comes—

DANA'S MOM: *(Overlapping)* That's not a good idea.

DANA: I have to do something!

DANA'S MOM: You're not going out there to drive around aimlessly in the state you're in. You need to calm down. The stress is not good for the baby.

DANA crosses to the view and looks out. Just looking.

DANA'S MOM: You said you called the police?

DANA: They practically laughed at me.

DANA'S MOM: I think by the end of the day, he'll be home and we'll all be laughing about this. You'll see.

DANA: It feels like the worst is about to happen. The very worst. And you're telling me I'll be laughing. Are you even hearing me? I'm telling you that I'm worried my husband might—

DANA'S MOM: Mike would never! *(Short beat)* You're letting your imagination run wild and—

DANA: WHERE IS HE?!

(Staying calm is not happening.)

DANA'S MOM: Take a sip of tea.

DANA: *(Just yelling out)* MIKE!

DANA'S MOM: Take a sip of tea, Dana.

DANA: MIIIIIIIIIIIKE!

DANA'S MOM: TAKE A DAMN SIP OF TEA!

(This surprises both DANA and DANA'S MOM. Interrupts DANA'S hysteria.)

(She tries to calm herself. Pulls herself back. Breathing)

(DANA'S MOM brings DANA the tea and just holds it out to her. DANA takes it. She slowly brings the cup to her mouth. She takes a sip.)

DANA'S MOM: Thank you.

(A few beats of quiet)

DANA: I'm so stupid, Mom. This whole mess…

DANA'S MOM: No.

DANA: I feel like I deserve this for being so stupid. I deserve this…

DANA'S MOM: Oh, honey…

DANA: And the truth…while Mike's been trying to actually do something to get us out of this mess, I've been waiting for it to just…to just go back to normal. Like it's just gonna magically work itself out. Or or or someone will save us. Who? I don't know. But I've been waiting for someone else to fix this. Of course Mike has felt alone.

DANA'S MOM: This is not an easy situation.

DANA: I left him alone. I did that.

DANA'S MOM: You're the just doing the best you can and…

DANA: I'm so stupid.

DANA'S MOM: Stop it.

DANA: Mom.

DANA'S MOM: Listen to me. You're not stupid. We all make mistakes. And right now you have that baby to think about so you can't spiral. Don't go to that dark place. Just be here. With me. With your baby. Be…here. And…breathe.

DANA: Breathe?

DANA'S MOM: Yes. Please. Just breathe.

(DANA *takes a deep breath in...lets it out.*)

(*A beat*)

DANA'S MOM: He's coming home. You have a bad feeling but I have a very strong good feeling. And you know my intuition. He's coming home.

DANA: You really think so.

DANA'S MOM: I do. He is coming home, Dana. He's coming home. Say it.

(*No response*)

DANA'S MOM: Say it.

DANA: He's coming home.

DANA'S MOM: Good. Again. Like you believe it.

DANA: He's coming home.

DANA'S MOM: He's coming home. Now what are you gonna do?

DANA: I'm gonna pack.

DANA'S MOM: Okay.

DANA: Will you help me?

DANA'S MOM: Of course.

DANA: When he comes home...I want him to see that I'm not afraid to let go.

Washing Feet

(*Lights up on* PREACHER PAULA *in plain dress. She sits in* MARCUS' *living room. He sits back in his chair, while she sits at the edge of hers, holding a glass of water. They don't talk to each other. She looks around. He watches her.*)

PREACHER PAULA: Vanessa really does have an eye for design. *(Beat)* She's at her mother's you say.

MARCUS: With the kids.

PREACHER PAULA: Just for a visit?

MARCUS: You could call it that.

(PREACHER PAULA takes a sip of her water.)

MARCUS: Well? *(Beat)* You gonna get to it?

PREACHER PAULA: Been doing some thinking, Marcus. Since your visit to my office. *(Beat)* You said some things that, well…
You remember when you first came to me wanting to volunteer your time to the church? Lots of people did that. Especially in those early days. But they would always be looking to usher or set up the chairs or help with a bake sale. Something like that. *(Beat)* Not you. "Preacher," you said. "I want you to give me the job that no one wants." Do you remember what I said to you?

(No response)

PREACHER PAULA: I said, "Well, Marcus. That would be cleaning the toilets. Why on earth would you want to clean the toilets?" And I'll never forget this. You said—

MARCUS: Because it's washing feet.

PREACHER PAULA: It's washing feet. *(Beat)* You wanted the job no one else would do because you wanted to emulate Jesus.

MARCUS: I'm surprised you remember that.

PREACHER PAULA: I was never the one who got you to believe, Marcus. The Holy Spirit did that for you. The path to Jesus is not an easy one. But you know that, don't you?

MARCUS: You got nineteen thousand other believers in Fort Lauderdale alone, Pastor. You don't need me.

PREACHER PAULA: No, please. Marcus, you cleaned those toilets because of Him. And now you help him carry the cross. The pain is more than you think you can handle. But I promise you. It will be worth it. One day. It might not look the way you thought it would or hoped it would. But don't you dare miss it by being angry.

(Beat)

(MARCUS *goes to exit.*)

PREACHER PAULA: Where are you going? *(She stands. Waits. Uncomfortable)*

(MARCUS *returns carrying a pair of latex gloves and a bucket filled with cleaning supplies: toilet bowl cleaner and a toilet brush.*)

MARCUS: We got toilets. *(He holds the bucket out to her. A beat)*

(PREACHER PAULA *takes the bucket from* MARCUS.)

PREACHER PAULA: How many toilets exactly do you have?

MARCUS: Just the two.

PREACHER PAULA: Okay. Yeah. I can do this.

MARCUS: No one's forcing you.

PREACHER PAULA: No. I'm doing this. It has been way too long since I washed anyone's feet. *(She puts on the gloves.)* Okay. Show me the way.

MARCUS: You can start with the kids' bathroom. This way.

(MARCUS *and* PREACHER PAULA *exit.*)

PREACHER PAULA: *(OS)* Oh sweet Jesus.

Robbie Helps Florence Find Her Way Home

(ROBBIE sits beside FLORENCE reading Psalm 27: 4-5
from her Bible. FLORENCE sleeps.

ROBBIE: "One thing I ask of the LORD, this is what I
seek: that I may dwell in the house of the LORD all the
days of my life, to gaze upon the beauty of the LORD
and to seek him in his temple. For in the day of trouble
he will keep me safe in his dwelling—."

(FLORENCE *makes a noise.* ROBBIE *stops.*)

ROBBIE: Nurse!

(FLORENCE *waves him off.*)

FLORENCE: No nurse. I don't like the nurse.

ROBBIE: You should rest.

FLORENCE: I was resting. You woke me up with your
reading.

ROBBIE: Sorry. I'll just… (*He gets up.*)

FLORENCE: Sit back down. I'm awake now.

ROBBIE: Okay.

(*A beat or two*)

FLORENCE: You trying to save my soul or something?

ROBBIE: No, I just…I thought…it's from your house.
This is your Bible.

(ROBBIE *shows* FLORENCE.)

FLORENCE: That was Martin's. He read a passage
every night. After he passed I thought I might take up
reading it.

ROBBIE: Do you?

FLORENCE: No. I just keep it by the bed.

ROBBIE: I never used to believe in the power of prayer
until this.

FLORENCE: What's that?

ROBBIE: *(A little louder)* The power of prayer.

FLORENCE: You been praying for me?

ROBBIE: Yes, ma'am. Every day.

FLORENCE: Why?

ROBBIE: Why?

FLORENCE: I didn't ask you to.

ROBBIE: Well, no. You don't have to ask. I felt like doing it.

FLORENCE: What are you praying for?

ROBBIE: That you live.

FLORENCE: Well, cut it out.

(ROBBIE takes this as a joke. He laughs.)

(Realizes it wasn't a joke. Stops)

ROBBIE: Mrs R? I just thought you should know…I'm done with that business. I told the Sheriff. It's not what I signed up for. I do not enjoy kicking people out of their homes. *(A beat)* I tried… Because I thought…if someone has to do it, better if it's me. See? I'm good in terrible situations. That's my life training. Terrible awful situations. One after another. That's when I thrive. But…I can't do it. Not this. I told the sheriff he should out right refuse to do any evictions anymore. Everybody needs to just take a breath. That's what I told him. I told him there's more to this than anyone knows. And we shouldn't be helping make more homeless. We should find a way to help. To give everyone some room. Take a stand. Take a breath. "Not my problem." That's what he said. Not. My. Problem.

(ROBBIE looks at FLORENCE. She pats his hand. A beat.)

ROBBIE: Mrs R? Why'd you have to go and do that? Why'd you have to...shoot yourself?

FLORENCE: Guess I didn't think it through—

ROBBIE: But you're gonna be all right. You're gonna live. That's what the doctors are sayin'. You're gonna live.

FLORENCE: Guess I shoulda used a revolver.

ROBBIE: That's...that's not funny.

(FLORENCE *cringes in pain.*)

FLORENCE: Sure doesn't feel like I missed. *(Beat)* So I'm gonna live?

ROBBIE: Well, until you die. Now's just not that time. So, yeah. You're gonna live.

FLORENCE: Where?

(A beat)

ROBBIE: Now, before you react I just want you to hear me out and then think about it. Okay?

FLORENCE: Before I react? I don't like the sound of this.

ROBBIE: See, I talked it over with Leila and—

FLORENCE: Oh no you didn't.

ROBBIE: And she said the same thing I did. It was her idea, actually. We both agree that you should come live with us.

FLORENCE: No, no, no, no, no, no, no, no, no, no/

(FLORENCE'S *chant of "No" continues and overlaps* ROBBIE.)

ROBBIE: Now, Mrs R, hear me out. I wish you'd just listen.

FLORENCE: No, no, no, no, no, no, no, no/

ROBBIE: Do you really have a choice?

FLORENCE: No, no, no—

ROBBIE: *(Strong)* It's already settled!

(FLORENCE stops. Quiet. A beat)

ROBBIE: Leila's got your room all ready. It's on the first floor so you won't have to use the stairs. The boys are just gonna share a room now.
Shoulda been that way from the beginning anyway. I shared a room with three brothers. That's what bunk beds are for.

FLORENCE: Robbie. I can't do that…I can't…I just want—

ROBBIE: You just want your house. I know. But the bank is gonna sell it to someone else now. And you're gonna live with us. Pain in the ass that you are.

(FLORENCE opens her mouth to speak. ROBBIE stops her.)

ROBBIE: Uh uh. You got plenty of time to think it over in here while you get yourself better. You need to heal that wound first.

(FLORENCE looks at ROBBIE, tears in her eyes.)

FLORENCE: Robbie…

ROBBIE: Boy, you don't give up, do you?—

FLORENCE: Thank you.

Letting Go

(DANA continues to pack with MOM's help.)

(DANA stops. She senses something. She turns and sees MIKE—)

DANA: *(Such relief)* Mike.

(DANA *rushes to* MIKE. *They cling to each other with utter relief with the realization that this moment is all that matters. They have each other.)*

(DANA *pulls back to see* MIKE's *face. They connect and say everything without saying anything. These lines could be said by either or both:)*

I'm sorry.

You scared me.

Don't ever leave me again.

(But they don't say that. Not with words, at least. Then…)

DANA: You're here.

MIKE: I'm here.

DANA: You're really here.

(MIKE *notices the boxes.)*

MIKE: You're packing.

DANA: Yeah. It's just a house. Right?

MIKE: *(I'm so fucking sorry)* Dana…

(DANA *hands* MIKE *the packing tape. [A lifeline])*

DANA: Here. This one's ready.

(MIKE *takes the tape and seals up the box.)*

(DANA *sits on it.)*

(He kneels in front of her. Puts his hands on her abdomen.)

MIKE: *(Suddenly crying)* I'm so sorry…

(MIKE *cries as* DANA *holds him.)*

DANA: I know. So am I.

MIKE: I'm so sorry…

DANA: It's okay. Shhhh… Hey. Mike. Hey…

(MIKE *looks up at* DANA.)

DANA: Why did the monkey fall out of the tree?

MIKE: Why?

DANA: Because he was dead.

(*A beat.* MIKE *kisses* DANA.)

(BUYERS *enter. Looking at the house*)

BUYER 1: It's perfect, baby.

BUYER 2: Our baby will sleep in that room.

BUYER 1: And you'll make love to me in front of that fireplace…

BUYER 2: On a soft rug.

BUYER 1: It feels like we've always lived here.

BUYER 2: Like we always will.

(MIKE *kisses* DANA *as though he's seeing her for the first time all over again.*)

(HUGO STORM *enters in on-camera mode.*)

HUGO STORM: Though the housing crisis continues to worsen and countless homeowners gasp for air as their dreams go up in smoke, for others the dream of owning a home will never die.

BUYER 1: I've always dreamt of living in a tree house. Perched on the skinny branches…

DANA'S MOM: I've been thinking it might be nice to have you live with us for a bit…

BUYER 2: With an endless view of the lights below.

DANA'S MOM: Just until you're back on your feet.

HUGO STORM: To be American is to dream.

BUYER 1: A house.

BUYER 2: A house.

ROBBIE: Consider it your home.

DANA'S MOM: Mi casa es su casa.

(PREACHER PAULA *is onstage dressed down.*)

PREACHER PAULA: Your faith is your home.

DANA'S MOM: We can help with the baby!

HUGO STORM: To own a home is to be American. The question is…

BUYER 2: Are we really doing this?

BUYER 1: Do you want to?

HUGO STORM: The question…

BUYER 2: More than anything.

HUGO STORM: Why?

DANA: We could live in an empty water drain…

MIKE: A balloon…

DANA: A drop of rain.

(Lights down)

END OF PLAY

www.ingramcontent.com/pod-product-compliance
Lightning Source LLC
Chambersburg PA
CBHW070020110426
42741CB00034B/2249